1,000,000 Books

are available to read at

Forgotten Books

———◇———

www.ForgottenBooks.com

———◇———

Read online
Download PDF
Purchase in print

ISBN 978-1-330-80768-2
PIBN 10108036

This book is a reproduction of an important historical work. Forgotten Books uses
state-of-the-art technology to digitally reconstruct the work, preserving the original format
whilst repairing imperfections present in the aged copy. In rare cases, an imperfection in
the original, such as a blemish or missing page, may be replicated in our edition. We do,
however, repair the vast majority of imperfections successfully; any imperfections that
remain are intentionally left to preserve the state of such historical works.

Forgotten Books is a registered trademark of FB &c Ltd.
Copyright © 2018 FB &c Ltd.
FB &c Ltd, Dalton House, 60 Windsor Avenue, London, SW19 2RR.
Company number 08720141. Registered in England and Wales.

For support please visit www.forgottenbooks.com

1 MONTH OF
FREE
READING

at

www.ForgottenBooks.com

---◆---

By purchasing this book you are eligible for one month membership to ForgottenBooks.com, giving you unlimited access to our entire collection of over 1,000,000 titles via our web site and mobile apps.

To claim your free month visit:

www.forgottenbooks.com/free108036

* Offer is valid for 45 days from date of purchase. Terms and conditions apply.

English
Français
Deutsche
Italiano
Español
Português

www.forgottenbooks.com

Mythology Photography **Fiction**
Fishing Christianity **Art** Cooking
Essays Buddhism Freemasonry
Medicine **Biology** Music **Ancient**
Egypt Evolution Carpentry Physics
Dance Geology **Mathematics** Fitness
Shakespeare **Folklore** Yoga Marketing
Confidence Immortality Biographies
Poetry **Psychology** Witchcraft
Electronics Chemistry History **Law**
Accounting **Philosophy** Anthropology
Alchemy Drama Quantum Mechanics
Atheism Sexual Health **Ancient History**
Entrepreneurship Languages Sport
Paleontology Needlework Islam
Metaphysics Investment Archaeology
Parenting Statistics Criminology
Motivational

The Elements of Speculation

BY

THOMAS GIBSON

Author of "Pitfalls of Speculation", "Cycles of Speculation", etc.

With a Suggestion as to a Measure for Relief from Periodical Money Stringency.

BY CHARLES F. M'ELROY.

The Gibson Publishing Company,

29 Broadway, New York

1913

A

Copyright, 1913, by
The Gibson Publishing Company.
All Rights Reserved.

CONTENTS

CHAPTER I.

Introduction.

For the sake of a clear understanding it may be well to define the meaning of the word "Speculation" as employed in this volume. There has been a widespread corruption of the term, particularly when applied to operations in securities. The popular understanding is that a speculator is one who gambles on margin, who buys what he cannot pay for, or sells what he does not own. The man who buys outright and pays for what he buys is called an investor. In both cases the terms are frequently misused. Any purchase of securities made because the stock or bond purchased is considered cheap and in hope of an advance in value and price, is a speculative purchase. It matters not whether the property so acquired is paid for in cash or a partial payment made in the form of a margin. Yet so hazy is the general opinion on this subject that the man who buys on margin and borrows the balance from his broker is called a speculator, while the man who buys outright and then hypothecates his certificates with his banker for a loan is called an investor. The process is exactly the same in both cases. The distinction is without a difference. If a purchase is made through a broker on margin, the broker must at once pay for the purchase in full, charging the unpaid balance to the customer as a loan. The actual certifictes are the broker's security just as they would become a bank's security in case they are made the basis of a loan.

If we wish to draw a knife edge between the two terms "speculation" and "investment," we must look upon everything purchased in the belief that higher prices will be realized later as a speculative venture, and confine the word "investment" to purchases made for income return alone, without reference to possible profits through accretion in value or price.

We are continually hearing warnings against speculation from rich men who have made their own fortunes in speculation—fortunes which could have been made in no other way—and from self-appointed public educators who have not the slightest conception of what they are talking about. They accomplish nothing. They could accomplish a great deal if, instead of issuing blanket warnings against all forms of speculation, they would point out the hopelessness of gambling on inadequate margins or following tips, charts or other *ignis fatuui* which lure the speculator to his undoing. If these mentors would impress their audiences with the fact that all the get-rich-quick devices masquerading as speculative opportunities are traps or dreams; that speculation means a correct forecasting of the future progress of a certain territory, or of the entire general business situation, or of a specific security, and that the accuracy of such forecasting was wholly dependent upon personal toil and study, they would confer a greater boon on society than by bawling to their followers to abjure speculation in any form and get rich saving their wages.

Speculation, whether it is in securities, real estate, groceries or whatever, must be conducted as a business, and when a man enters that business he must equip himself with intimate knowledge of its character and possibilities. I do not hesitate, after many years of observation and experience, to state that no large fortune can be made in a brief period of time in the speculative world, and that no fortune of any kind can be made in any period of time by speculating blindly on tips or information. People have grown suddenly rich by discovering gold mines, etc., but that is accident rather than speculation. If any large fortune is ever made in speculation in a brief period, it is merely an exception which proves a rule.

In former works I have pointed out in a general way the errors and the possibilities of speculative ventures and offered suggestions as to correct methods. In this volume I will take up in more detail the principal fundamental factors governing security price movements and endeavor to show how such factors may be examined and weighed expeditiously and accurately. It is realized that the subject is too broad for a complete discussion in the limits of a single volume, but it is hoped that what is suggested will be found helpful and will act as an incentive to further personal examination and study.

CHAPTER II.

The Anteriority of Security Prices.

In conducting speculative ventures intelligently, one of the most common errors is the failure to understand or give due consideration to the anteriority of security prices. Because of this neglect, or lack of understanding, many people become disgusted and claim that the wide swings of security prices cannot be reasonably forecasted; that price movements are irrational, and that study is of no avail. This is all wrong. There are frequently intermediate spasms which carry prices above or below values, but these are always temporary and such artificial disturbances are quickly followed by a return of prices to their proper relation with values. It appears rather anomalous that so many people should rail against these periods of undue depression or inflation when we reflect that our greatest speculative opportunities are present when prices and values are temporarily divorced. The hiatus may be due to manipulation, to scarcity or plethora of money, or to other causes; but when these influences are removed, prices will seek values as surely as water seeks its own level.

The stock market moves ahead of actual events. It is pushed either up or down by the force of buying or selling by the important interests which foresee coming prosperity or depression. In 1905 we had an advancing market in anticipation of good times ahead. In 1907 we had a great decline in stock prices and a boom year in business. In 1908 and 1909 we had poor business and an advancing stock market. Wise and farsighted men bought in 1905 and sold in 1906. They sold to the large class of operators who grow excited at the sight of activity marketwise, who are encouraged by tangible evidences of business prosperity and who do not stop to reflect that all that is good has already been discounted by the high prices of securities. These buyers do not understand the precession of security prices, or if they do understand it, they do not properly employ their knowledge.

We must, therefore, begin our study with the assumption that it is impossible to *speculate* on what is *known*; that security prices always move ahead of events, and that in order to succeed we must give our attention to the correct forecasting of future happenings. The man who attempts to speculative on "tips", or "inside information", or "tape reading", or in any other way without a special study of the more important basic factors might as well throw his money away and be done with it. It may be contended that it is impossible to study or correctly foresee great fundamental factors which are as yet unknown, but not so. By a careful study of precedent and of future prospeets as indicated by present conditions, we may arrive at correct conclusions with a surprising degree of accuracy. It is not meant to say that we cannot gain anything from certain forms of open information, or from a scrutiny of the technical position of stocks, or the character of buying and selling. All these may be of use as our education progresses, but they are of minor importance. If our basic views are correct, and if we operate reasonably without asking or expecting too much from the market, no intermediate reversals can injure us and our hopes of profit will eventually be realized. If, on the other hand, we ignore the basic factors or form careless and incorrect conclusions, nothing can save us.

There are certain important fundamentals bearing on security prices which are responsible for all great advances or declines. What these factors are and how we may examine and read them with the greatest facility and accuracy, I will endeavor to explain in this volume.

One important suggestion may be offered. In conducting examinations it will be found that our greatest aid is derived from precedent. It goes without saying that a normal growth must be allowed for in many cases. Production of minerals, agricultural products, railway earnings, etc., should gradually keep pace with increased population and it is important that we determine whether such growth is normal, subnormal or abnormal, either generally or in specific instances. This is not a difficult task. The greatest danger in consulting precedent lies in the very common practice of examining too brief a period and forming conclusions on entirely insufficient grounds. Comparisons of one month with a preceding month are usually ridiculous. There are certain seasons of the year when prices of money naturally rise and fall, certain seasons when railroad traffic is light or heavy, and so through a long line of factors. And comparisons of one year with another are not much better. An abnormal year of production of wheat, or of railroad earnings, or whatever, may be followed by a recession as compared with that abnormal year, and by this careless method of reckoning odious comparisons are frequently drawn. The railroad earnings of a certain year may appear unfavorable by contrast with the preceding year, but may appear just the reverse by comparisons with all other preceding years. As the value of precedent is largely dependent on history repeating itself when similar conditions exist, we should, whenever an abnormal deviation from the line of natural growth or accretion is apparent, seek the *reason* for such departure, and when that reason is found, it will be easy to determine whether such causes are existent or non-existent now, and so our deductions will be correctly based.

There is a tendency on the part of students of speculative probabilities to try to make their examinations too exhaustive. This is commendable when applied to the statistical examination of a specific property, but in determining the long swings of security prices in general, we may concentrate our attention on a few important fundamentals and give only secondary consideration to minor factors. Students who wish to make their examinations and deductions very thorough are frequently found wandering about in a bewildering jungle of figures and precedents, some of which contradict others, and the efforts to reconcile the whole only result in confusion. This form of study also leads very frequently to the attaching of undue importance to insignificant or interdependent factors. The course of the security markets is dependent largely upon the general prosperity of the country or, more broadly speaking, the general prosperity of the civilized world. The two most important basic factors making for prosperity are good crops and satisfactory money conditions. Satisfactory money conditions are dependent to a great extent on the crops and our foreign trade. If we scrutinize these dominant influences carefully we will find that our time is employed to the greatest advantage. Almost all other influences are merely offshoots of one or all the three factors mentioned. It is found that in twenty-five years only one instance occurred where the stock market did not reflect good or bad crops in its movements. We cannot, however, wait until the outcome of the harvests is a known quantity, for the market, moving ahead of events, will have discounted the good or bad results before they are apparent. Thus, in our year of greatest cereal and cotton production (1906) a very large advance occurred during July and August. When the large crops became a matter of history their effect had been duly measured and discounted. The same thing has been true in almost all similar cases.

The speculative rewards go to those who, by assiduous study and intelligent deduction, obtain a clear perspective of the probable future

CHAPTER III.

Crops.

So many other things are dependent on the products of the soil that the crops may easily be classed as the greatest of our fundamentals. The products of mines and forests are important and require examination from time to time in order to ascertain if the supply is keeping pace with demand, or if we are over or under-producing in certain quarters, but mines and forests do not require the same attention and investigation as do the agricultural products, as they are not subject to severe annual fluctuations through climatic conditions, insect ravages or the other ills that plant life is heir to.

Each year we draw from the soil through farm products from eight to nine billion dollars more or less. If the amount is distinctly less because of small crops, we are seriously affected in numerous ways; commodity prices may be higher because of the shortage, but higher prices will not cure the troubles arising from short crops. Our exportable surplus is smaller; the high prices between consumers and producers at home is merely swapping dollars; railroad traffic is reduced; labor is not fully employed; the masses suffer because of high prices. Large yields at low prices are very much to be preferred to small yields at high prices. A good many observers are apt to fall into the error of thinking that the ideal condition is a large yield at high prices, but such conditions are usually due to very short crops in other parts of the world and such a state of affairs acts as a boomerang, for the purchasing power of the world is reduced by the payment of high prices for the necessities of life, and our securities and manufactures suffer accordingly. Normal conditions, the world over, is the ideal state of affairs.

The man who undertakes to study crop conditions and prospects will find a world of information at his command. There are several good trade organs which gather and distribute the news of progress and probabilities; the government furnishes frequent reports during the season and much other valuable literature from time to time. Railroads and large business concerns gather statistics annually, many of which are available to the public, while brokerage houses and grain dealers employ their own experts for the benefit of their clients. There are also good books of a technical character which clear up many perplexing questions. Exhaustive statistical records can be had for little or nothing.

Unfortunately there is also a great deal of misinformation on the subject. People who are interested in advancing or depressing the prices of securities or commodities circulate misleading or false reports and even go so far as to employ experts who bias their reports according to a dictated policy. A good many farmers and planters who allow their cupidity to override their integrity make a practice of exploiting disaster and claiming crop damage on the theory that this will influence prices and benefit them accordingly. The false reports are not convincing, however, if proper attention is given to the study of the subject, and it is seldom the case that conscientious students who make their examinations comprehensive, are far out of the way in their estimates. It will not do to take much for granted, as we will quickly discover when we look at the great variations between two or more estimates of the same crop, published simultaneously. One may be extravagantly high and another extravagantly low.

The most widely used estimates and reports are those issued by the Department of Agriculture. The most important of these documents are a weekly weather report issued on Tuesday of each week and monthly reports of acreage and condition of all important crops. These exhibits are published in the following months:

April—Condition of winter wheat and rye.

May—Acreage and condition of winter wheat and rye, condition of meadows and spring pastures, spring ploughing and abandoned winter wheat acreage.

June—Condition of winter wheat, spring wheat, rye, barley, oats, clover and rice; average condition of spring pastures, apples and peaches.

July—Acreage and condition of corn; condition of winter and spring wheat, winter and spring rye, oats and barley, potatoes and tobacco, clover, timothy, apples and peaches.

August—Condition of spring wheat, corn, rye, oats, barley, tobacco, and acreage and condition of hay.

September—Condition of spring wheat, corn, tobacco and fruits. Also condition of winter wheat, rye, oats and barley at harvest.

October—Yield per acre of wheat, rye, oats and barley. Average condition of corn.

November—Average yield of corn, tobacco, etc., as compared with preceding year.

December—Acreage and condition of winter wheat and rye.

Other reports are issued in January and February giving general miscellaneous crop statistics.

The reports on cereals are customarily issued on the eighth day of the month, showing acreage or condition or both, as of the last day of the preceding month. It is frequently necessary to give consideration to changed conditions in the interval which elapses between the date of compilation and the date of publication. For example, a low condition may be shown because of drought, and this may be improved by several days of precipitation. It will be observed that the three months from June first to September first, is the most important period for our growing crops. In the three months of June, July and August, the greatest damage occurs from dry weather or excessive rainfall. Corn and cotton are also affected by the date of the first killing frost. No fixed line can be drawn as to the approximate date of danger from frost, as an early spring may bring the crop out of danger at an earlier date, or vice versa. Late spring planting and an early killing frost would almost certainly work serious injury.

The principal cereal crops which are to be considered as to their bearing on business conditions and security prices are wheat, corn and oats. Let us first examine the condition, acreage and production of these products for the last ten years as shown by the reports of the Department of Agriculture.

TABLE I.

Showing Condition of Wheat, Corn and Oats on the First of the Months Named—1902 to 1911 Inclusive.

	WINTER WHEAT					CORN			
	Apr.	May	June	July	Sept.*	June	July	Aug.	Sept.
02....	78.7	76.4	76.1	77.0	80.0	95.4	92.4	89.7	...
03....	97.3	92.6	82.2	78.8	74.7	95.9	82.5	77.1	...
04....	76.5	76.5	77.7	78.7	...	93.4	93.7	87.5	66.2
05....	91.6	92.5	85.5	82.7	...	93.7	91.0	89.7	87.3
06....	89.1	91.0	82.7	85.6	...	93.4	91.4	86.9	83.4
7....	89.9	82.9	77.4	78.3	...	88.7	87.2	79.4	77.1
08....	91.3	89.0	86.0	80.6	...	95.0	89.4	80.7	77.6
09....	82.2	83.5	80.7	82.4	...	95.2	82.7	91.6	83.6
10....	80.8	82.1	80.0	81.5	...	92.8	61.6	61.0	63.1
11....	83.3	86.1	80.4	76.8	...	94.6	73.8	59.8	56.7

	SPRING WHEAT				OATS			
	July	Aug.	Sept.	Oct.	June	July	Aug.	Sept.
02....	87.5	86.5	84.3	79.6	90.6	92.1	89.4	87.2
03....	79.4	78.7	80.1	80.8	85.5	84.3	79.5	75.7
04....	86.4	87.3	84.6	83.9	89.2	89.8	86.6	85.6
05....	87.3	89.0	89.5	89.2	92.9	92.1	90.8	90.3
06....	87.5	88.1	90.0	90.1	85.9	84.0	82.8	81.9
07....	80.2	82.8	80.2	78.0	81.6	81.0	75.6	65.5
08....	82.8	82.5	79.4	77.8	92.9	85.7	76.8	69.7
09....	89.3	84.4	74.6	73.8	98.7	88.3	85.5	83.8
10....	85.4	79.3	78.2	80.3	91.0	82.2	81.5	83.3
11....	80.1	69.6	70.3	70.4	85.7	68.8	65.7	64.5

*Includes winter and spring.

TABLE II.

Showing Acreage of Wheat, Corn and Oats— 1902 to 1911 Inclusive.

	Wheat		Corn	Oats
	Spring Acres	Winter Acres	Acres	Acres
1902—	17,620,998	28,581,426	94,043,613	28,653,144
1903—	16,954,457	32,510,510	88,091,993	27,638,126
1904—	17,209,020	26,865,855	92,231,581	27,842,669
1905—	17,990,061	29,864,018	94,011,369	28,046,746
1906—	17,705,868	29,599,961	96,737,581	30,958,768
1907—	17,079,000	28,132,000	99,031,000	31,837,000
1908—	17,208,000	30,349,000	101,788,000	32,344,000
1909—	18,393,000	28,330,000	108,771,000	33,204,000
1910—	19,778,000	29,427,000	114,002,000	35,288,000
1911—	20,381,000	29,162,000	105,825,000	37,763,000

TABLE III.

Showing Production of Wheat, Corn and Oats—
1902 to 1911 Inclusive (Bushels)

Year	Wheat	Corn	Oats
1902	670,063,000	2,523,648,000	987,843,000
1903	637,822,000	2,244,177,000	784,094,000
1904	522,400,000	2,467,481,000	894,596,000
1905	692,979,000	2,707,994,000	953,216,000
1906	735,261,000	2,927,416,000	964,904,000
1907	634,087,000	2,592,320,000	754,443,000
1908	664,602,000	2,668,651,000	807,156,000
1909	737,189,000	2,772,376,000	1,007,353,000
1910	695,443,000	3,125,713,000	1,126,765,000
1911	621,338,000	2,531,458,000	922,298,000

In examining Table 1, the first noticeable fact
is that there is *normal* deterioration in condition after the first report. This is particularly
pronounced in spring wheat. Until very recently the disregarding of this normal deterioration has caused much confusion and varia-
tion in estimates of final production. One
statistician would take the condition as shown
in the first report, arrive at the indicated production per acre, subtract the abandoned acreage, when given, and multiply by the remain-
ing acreage. It is plain that this would, in a
majority of cases, indicate a much larger yield
than would be harvested. Others attempted to
allow for deterioration according to their own
ideas, and each estimate was different from the
others. In 1911 the government, for the first
time, adopted a method of expressing quantitative estimates which will no doubt come
into more or less universal use in a short time.
This method is to take the deterioration from
the date of each report to the end of the growing season, average it for a number of preceding years and allow for the average amount of

falling off in the estimate of final yield. Such estimates can never be reduced to an exact science but the plan employed is as good as any so far suggested. Hereafter we will arrive at a quantitative estimate each month which will not be reduced if normal deterioration occurs. The crop indicated will be shown each month until it is harvested.

An explanation of the form and meaning of the monthly reports is given as follows by the Department of Agriculture.

INTERPRETATION OF ESTIMATES OF CONDITION AS EXPRESSED IN PERCENTAGES OF THE NORMAL.

The conditions of various crops is estimated periodically during the growing season by the Department of Agriculture. These estimates are expressed in the form of a percentage, the base, or 100 per cent, being termed a *"NORMAL" CONDITION.*

Three inquiries are often made as to such condition reports, namely: (1) What is a *NORMAL CONDITION?* (2) What yield is indicated by a normal condition? and (3) What is the method or formula for interpreting a given estimate of condition in terms of indicated production; in other words, with a given condition, how is the indicated production determined?

A NORMAL CONDITION may be defined as a condition that will produce *A NORMAL YIELD,* if such condition is maintained until harvest. *BUT WHAT IS A NORMAL YIELD?*

Most farmers know from experience approximately what their fields ought to produce, with the usual mode of farming, with normal weather conditions, and without unusual loss, disease, insects, or other injurious influences. A yield under such favorable, though not extraordinary conditions would be a normal yield, which is more than an average yield but less than a maximum possible yield. A condition which may produce a normal yield, as thus described, is a normal, or 100 per cent condition.

A normal yield for one farm or section may vary from that for another. On one field a normal yield per acre of corn might be 80 bushels, and on another field 12 bushels. A normal yield of corn for one State is more than 40 bushels per acre, for another State it is less than 14 bushels.

THE CONDITION OF A CROP at a given date is expressed by the percentage of a normal yield which may be produced if no change in the condition or status of the crop occur from the given date to the time of harvest. For example, if the condition of the wheat crop on June 1 were such that, with no change in condition —that is, normal influences from that date to harvest— only three-fourths of a normal yield could be expected, the condition would be reported as 75 per cent; if only one-half a normal crop could be expected, the condition would be reported as 50 per cent; if 10 per cent more than a normal yield could be expected, the condition would be reported as 110.

THE NORMAL YIELD OF A CROP FOR A STATE OR FOR THE UNITED STATES MAY BE DETERMINED approximately in a practical way by multiplying the average yield per acre for any number of years by 100 and dividing the product by the average, for the same years, of the condition of the crop at or near the time of harvest. For example, the condition of corn is reported the last time as of October 1; if the average condition of the crop on October 1 for the ten years 1899-1908 was 80 per cent, and if the average yield per acre in the ten years 1899-1908 was 28 bushels per acre, it may be assumed that 80 per cent of normal condition will produce 28 bushels; therefore, by proportion, 100 per cent will be 35 bushels; that is,

$$28 \times 100 \div 80 = 35.$$

An average for five years, instead of ten, or any number of years, may be used for this comparison, but with slightly varying results.

This method cannot give a precise equivalent of 100 per cent, because a change sometimes occurs in a crop after the date of the last condition report and before harvest, and also because the data used are estimates and subjects to errors of judgment. But for practical purposes the method is valid for obtaining approximations.

A normal yield being known, it is a simple process TO REDUCE ANY GIVEN CONDITION FIGURE TO ITS YIELD EQUIVALENT; that is, multiply the normal yield by the condition figure, and divide by 100. For example, if the condition of corn is 80 per cent, where a normal or 100 yield is 35 bushels, the indicated yield would be 80 per cent of 35 bushels, or 28 bushels (80 × 35 ÷ 100).

The yield obtained by the method thus described is the yield which may be expected providing the condition of the crop does not decline or improve after the date of the estimate. But as a crop advances to maturity some portion of it usually suffers from some damaging influences, causing a decline in condition.

TO FORECAST THE PROBABLE OUTCOME OF A CROP ON THE BASIS OF THE CONDITION AT A GIVEN DATE, ACCOUNT IS TAKEN OF THE AVERAGE CHANGE (USUALLY DECLINE) IN CONDITION FROM THE GIVEN DATE TO THE TIME OF HARVEST, it is assumed that the change in condition to the time of harvest will be the same as an average change. In other words, it is assumed that the probable yield will be in the same ratio to the average yield as the condition of the crop on a given date is to the average condition on that date.

For example, on the basis of a ten-year average, suppose the average condition of corn in the United States on July 1 is 87 per cent, the average yield is 27 bushels. Suppose the condition on July 1 is 75; it is then assumed that the probable yield (?) will be to 27 bushels as 75 is to 87, which is

$$\frac{27 \times 75}{87} = 23.3 \text{ (bushels)}$$

That is, multiply the average yield by the indicated condition at the given date and divide by the average condition on the same date.

The "normal" yield per acre (decade 1899-1908) of various crops for the United States (based upon the ten-year average of the percentage of normal condition of crop at or near the time of harvest and the average yield per acre in the same years) is found to be approximately as follows: Winter wheat, 17.5 bushels; spring wheat, 17.5 bushels; corn, 32.6; oats, 36.8; barley, 30.8; rye, 18.1; buckwheat, 21.8; potatoes, 118.1 bushels tobacco, 968.8 pounds; cotton, 280.1 pounds; rice, 35.5 bushels; flaxseed (five-year average), 11.9 bushels.

THE "NORMAL" YIELD OF CROPS PER ACRE, THAT IS, THE YIELD PER ACRE WHICH IS EXPECTED UNDER NORMAL CONDITIONS, IS GRADUALLY INCREASING.

It will be noted from the condition tables that a high or low condition in the early months does not always insure a large or small crop. This may be due to weather conditions, insect, rust or smut damage, small initial acreage or abandoned acreage, all of which must be watched and taken into consideration.

In making allowance for abandoned acreage, it is necessary to reflect that there is always some abandonment and that such acreage does not represent a total loss, as in most cases it is utilized for the production of other cereals which require later planting.

After the initial reports of acreage, condition, abandoned acreage, etc., are published, the daily progress of crops may be followed more satisfactorily by reference to climatic changes, and the published reports of precipitation and temperature, than by attention to crop-killing stories from different isolated localities. There is no such thing as a perfect crop season. There is always some spotted damage, and this so impresses the man who reports it that its importance is exaggerated. Hail storms can cut a field all to pieces, but hail storms are always local. Insect damage has been vigorously exploited almost every year, but the fact remains that the loss in cereals from this cause is only trifling. Serious damage seldom occurs from late frosts in the *spring* of the year. Floods have at times caused serious damage, but very rarely—only once in recent years(1904). The greatest and most widespread losses are due to weather conditions, and it is by a study of these changes that we can arrive at the safest and most accurate conclusions.

The most important states in the production of wheat, corn and oats are shown in the following tables in the order of their importance. I have taken the year 1910 for the illustrations instead of 1911 for two reasons—first, that 1910 was more nearly a normal year than 1911; second, the production figures of 1911 are still subject to revision. The object sought in these four tables is to show the relative importance of leading states as to acreage. The casual observer is apt to be misled by crop-killing advices unless he is conversant with the facts. He may hear, for example, that the spring wheat crop of Iowa is a failure and be impressed by that statement, but when he observes that Iowa raises about 7,000,000 bushels of spring wheat, while Minnesota raises about 94,000,000 bushels, the matter is viewed in another light.

Table IV.

WINTER WHEAT.

(States raising 10,000,000 bushels or more.)

State	Acreage 1910	Production 1910 (Bushels)
Kansas	4,300,000	61,060,000
Indiana	2,627,000	40,981,000
Nebraska	2,100,000	34,650,000
Illinois	2,100,000	31,500,000
Ohio	1,944,000	31,493,000
Pennsylvania	1,556,000	27,697,000
Oklahoma	1,556,000	25,363,000
Missouri	1,821,000	25,130,000
Texas	1,252,000	18,780,000
California	950,000	17,100,000
Michigan	869,000	15,642,000

State	Acreage 1910	Production 1910 (Bushels)
Washington.........	676,000	13,858,000
Maryland	794,000	13,816,000
Oregon	467,000	11,068,000
Tennessee	910,000	10,647,000
New York	444,000	10,523,000
Virginia	795,000	10,176,000
Other States	4,266,000	64,560,000
Total.............	29,427,000	464,044,000

Table V.

SPRING WHEAT.

(States raising over 5,000,000 bushels.)

State	Acreage 1910	Production 1910 (Bushels)
Minnesota	5,880,000	94,080,000
South Dakota	3,650,000	46,720,000
North Dakota	7,221,000	36,105,000
Washington	810,000	11,745,000
Iowa	350,000	7,315,000
Colorado	289,000	6,329,000
Oregon	297,000	5,346,000
Other States	1,281,000	23,759,000
Total.............	19,778,000	231,399,000

Table VI.
CORN.
(States raising over 10,000,000 bushels.)

State	Acreage 1910	Production 1910 (Bushels)
Illinois	10,609,000	414,812,000
Iowa	9,473,000	343,870,000
Missouri	8,300,000	273,900,000
Nebraska	8,000,000	206,400,000
Indiana	5,120,000	201,216,000
Texas	8,800,000	181,280,000
Kansas	8,900,000	169,100,000
Ohio	3,960,000	144,540,000
Kentucky	3,630,000	105,270,000
Tennessee	3,720,000	96,348,000
Oklahoma	5,772,000	92,352,000
Arkansas	2,884,000	69,216,000
Michigan	2,100,000	68,040,000
Mississippi	3,232,000	66,256,000
Georgia	4,532,000	65,714,000
Pennsylvania	1,586,000	65,026,000
Alabama	3,524,000	63,432,000
Louisiana	2,493,000	58,835,000
North Carolina	3,072,000	57,139,000
Minnesota	1,724,000	56,375,000
Virginia	2,142,000	54,621,000
South Dakota	2,162,000	54,050,000
Wisconsin	1,575,000	51,188,000
South Carolina	2,418,000	44,733,000
New York	680,000	26,044,000
West Virginia	920,000	23,920,000
Maryland	710,000	23,785,000
New Jersey	290,000	10,440,000
Other States	1,674,000	37,811,000
Total.............	114,002,000	3,125,713,000

Table VII.

OATS.

(States raising over 10,000,000 bushels.)

State	Acreage 1910	Production 1910 (Bushels)
Iowa	4,800,000	181,440,000
Illinois	4,500,000	171,000,000
Minnesota	2,736,000	78,523,000
Nebraska	2,650,000	74,200,000
Wisconsin	2,320,000	69,136,000
Ohio	1,765,000	65,658,000
Indiana	1,850,000	65,490,000
Michigan	1,505,000	51,170,000
Kansas	1,400,000	46,620,000
New York	1,338,000	46,161,000
Pennsylvania	998,000	35,130,000
South Dakota	1,525,000	35,075,000
Missouri	780,000	26,208,000
Texas	695,000	24,325,000
Oklahoma	632,000	23,068,000
Montana	350,000	13,300,000
North Dakota	1,628,000	11,396,000
Oregon	302,000	10,419,000
Other States	3,514,000	98,446,000
Total...........	35,288,000	1,126,765,000

Abnormal or subnormal temperatures or precipitation in certain months of the growing season do not always indicate probable damage. A great deal depends upon what follows or what has preceded such conditions. A dry fall followed by only normal rainfall during the growing season may work havoc with spring wheat and other cereals. The soil has not stored up its usual amount of moisture, and abnormally heavy rainfall will be necessary for a large crop. A dry spring followed by copious rains sometimes produces the best general crops, as the roots go down seeking for water and the stand is firm and good. On the other hand, a wet spring followed by insufficient moisture is very bad, as the roots spread out laterally and when the dry weather comes they have only a coating of dust to protect them. Cool weather in a period of drought is always helpful, as it greatly reduces evaporation. A wet fall and a heavy snow covering in the winter months is always a most promising condition, unless there is too much alternate freezing and thawing in February and March. A fair knowledge of soil conditions and a constant and intelligent examination of precipitation and temperatures will be found essential to correct estimates of probable production.

It has been stated that some improvement has been made in the methods of calculation offered by the Government, but there is much to be desired. The trouble lies in the necessity of adopting some system of averages on which to base estimates. It is impossible to do this satisfactorily in a case where each year's results are subject to irregular fluctuations and specific changes. It is also impossible to make anything more than machines out of the accountants and statisticians who handle the figures, and this leads at times to results which do not square with reason. Estimates founded either on average production per acre or average condition, frequently turn out very badly. Two illustrations of this may be offered.

In estimating the spring wheat crop of 1911 the Department of Agriculture based the probable crop on production of 13.7 bushels per acre, simply multiplying the acreage by 13.7. This figure, 13.7, was obtained by adding the production per acre for the preceding five years and dividing by 5. But the spring wheat crop of 1910 was a failure (only 11.7 bushels per acre) and this single figure, the lowest in years, brought down the general average too much. The average production for the five years preceding 1910 was 14.1 bushels per acre. If we go back for ten years and eliminate two years of absolute crop failure and one year of unusually large production, we still have over 14 bushels per acre.

Even more misleading is the method of averaging condition and subtracting for socalled normal deterioration. Under this method we find that in the last ten years the condition of winter wheat has averaged slightly lower on July 1 than on June 1; but in seven years out of the ten conditions improved, and in three years there was enough deterioration to offset all the improvement. But that is not the worst of it. The deterioration is traceable to a specific cause, about the only cause, in fact, which could cause deterioration in winter wheat in a harvest month. The cause is a late spring. Harvest is deferred and the standing grain suffers. How absurd it appears to apply this law of averages to a year where the specific cause is absent and possibility of damage in June cancelled by an early harvest.

There is only one way to employ the figures given by the Government or private statisticians, and that is to make each report a law unto itself. Determine whether or not planting has been early or late, the condition of the soil, etc., and keep track of precipitation and temperatures from week to week. Use the figures of acreage and condition only as a tentative basis and do what the accountants cannot be expected to do, *i. e.*, modify arithmetical calculations by employing reason and common sense.

One of the greatest aids to correct conclusions in the periods between Government crop reports is a daily examination of temperatures and precipitation. This receives too little attention; and, strange as it may appear, no compilation has ever been arranged showing normal precipitation and temperatures in all important States by months. This omission is supplied by the following tables:

Georgia	44.5	46.7	57.2	63.1	72.1	78.0	80.1	79.2	74.6	64.2	54.1
Illinois	26.4	26.9	40.4	51.7	62.6	72.3	75.6	73.7	66.8	54.4	40.5
Indiana	27.8	28.5	41.1	51.5	62.6	71.5	75.6	73.1	68.8	54.7	41.8
Iowa	19.3	19.2	34.0	48.5	60.1	68.8	73.4	71.8	63.7	51.9	35.9
Kansas	29.5	29.8	42.8	54.8	64.3	72.8	77.8	77.1	69.2	57.2	42.6
Kentucky	35.2	35.1	46.2	56.0	65.7	74.1	77.3	76.3	70.2	57.9	46.0
Louisiana	50.3	51.9	61.1	66.9	73.8	81.6	81.6	81.5	77.4	67.5	58.5
Maryland	32.3	31.6	41.8	51.4	62.7	70.7	75.4	73.3	67.4	55.5	44.2
Michigan	20.4	18.3	29.0	50.9	53.8	63.8	68.4	66.6	60.3	48.6	35.6
Minnesota	9.7	10.8	25.1	42.5	54.6	64.2	68.6	66.6	58.1	45.6	29.0
Mississippi	46.2	47.5	57.7	64.3	72.2	78.8	80.8	80.5	75.5	64.1	61.5
Missouri	31.2	31.1	43.5	55.0	65.2	73.4	76.0	76.3	69.4	58.0	44.2
Montana	19.7	21.5	30.2	42.6	51.9	59.0	65.9	63.9	55.4	45.5	31.7
Nebraska	23.6	24.0	36.4	49.3	59.4	68.6	73.9	72.9	64.4	51.5	36.8
New Jersey	29.7	30.0	38.0	49.1	60.4	69.3	73.9	71.9	65.8	54.2	43.1
New York	21.7	20.4	31.1	43.6	56.0	64.7	69.1	66.6	60.7	49.0	36.8
North Carolina	40.1	41.2	50.3	57.3	67.7	74.3	77.3	76.5	70.8	59.9	49.7
North Dakota	5.6	6.7	21.0	41.4	53.0	62.3	67.3	66.1	56.0	43.6	26.2
Ohio	27.8	26.4	39.0	49.3	61.1	69.3	73.8	71.7	65.6	53.4	40.8
Oklahoma	38.3	38.1	51.3	60.0	67.7	76.0	80.3	80.9	73.3	61.6	50.1
Oregon	35.4	37.8	42.5	48.9	54.2	59.5	66.0	65.3	57.8	51.2	42.8
Pennsylvania	27.8	24.8	37.2	48.0	59.7	69.6	72.2	70.2	63.9	51.8	40.4
South Carolina	45.7	45.6	55.5	61.7	71.5	77.9	79.9	79.2	74.1	63.0	54.1
South Dakota	15.7	16.0	29.2	45.5	55.8	65.9	71.6	70.4	60.5	48.6	31.7
Tennessee	38.0	39.5	49.2	58.2	67.2	75.0	77.3	76.5	70.6	59.0	55.0
Texas	48.4	49.0	59.8	66.6	73.3	80.2	82.5	82.4	77.1	67.4	56.9
Virginia	35.3	35.1	45.3	53.3	64.3	71.7	75.7	74.2	68.2	56.5	46.0
Washington	32.9	35.9	41.1	49.3	55.6	61.0	67.1	66.2	59.1	48.5	41.1
West Virginia	31.9	30.5	43.1	50.6	62.3	69.2	73.6	72.6	66.5	54.9	43.0
Wisconsin	14.7	15.3	28.4	43.8	54.9	64.7	69.0	69.0	60.2	47.9	33.1

Georgia		.29	4.94	3.52	3.47	4.52	5.16	5.74	3.62	2.64	2.70
Illinois	2.45	2.36	3.16	2.29	4.21	3.74	3.87	3.15	3.41	2.11	2.62
Indiana	2.90	2.89	3.89	3.11	3.64	4.08	3.12	3.37	2.76	2.42	3.65
Iowa	1.05	1.02	1.92	2.83	4.50	4.52	4.44	3.99	3.41	2.05	1.39
Kansas	.72	1.04	1.53	2.68	4.24	4.55	4.16	3.08	2.88	1.69	0.82
Kentucky	4.01	3.57	5.01	3.65	3.94	4.34	4.13	3.25	2.72	2.32	3.7
Louisiana	4.43	5.08	4.66	4.43	4.42	5.3	5.42	4.73	2.61	2.91	4.45
Maryland	3.05	3.33	3.75	3.27	3.83	4.03	4.75	4.25	3.29	3.11	2.95
Michigan	2.08	1.81	2.12	2.03	3.32	3.02	3.37	2.42	3.17	2.72	2.48
Minnesota	.62	.70	1.42	2.27	3.60	4.25	3.61	3.27	3.05	2.33	1.21
Mississippi	4.81	4.93	5.91	4.41	3.84	3.62	4.8	4.58	3.38	2.26	3.55
Missouri	2.44	2.29	3.20	3.68	4.95	4.78	4.41	3.7	3.65	2.43	2.48
Montana	0.85	0.89	1.03	1.32	2.99	2.73	1.45	0.92	1.72	1.10	1.11
Nebraska	0.5	0.67	0.97	2.55	3.64	3.85	3.64	2.94	2.23	1.65	0.6
New Jersey	3.70	3.92	4.01	3.56	3.85	3.76	4.83	4.65	3.84	3.53	3.5
New York	2.87	2.78	3.17	2.52	2.56	4.01	4.30	3.90	3.32	3.49	2.77
North Carolina	3.86	4.75	4.67	3.84	4.35	5.0	6.34	5.65	1.54	3.49	2.88
North Dakota	0.52	0.48	0.90	1.49	2.41	3.59	2.48	2.97	1.49	1.17	0.66
Ohio	2.77	2.6	3.52	2.81	3.63	3.95	4.1	3.16	2.73	2.25	2.85
Oklahoma	1.19	1.12	2.26	3.1	5.67	4.29	3.32	2.80	2.89	2.57	2.02
Oregon	4.74	4.6	4.64	2.95	2.17	1.60	0.23	0.6	1.78	2.69	5.50
Pennsylvania	3.32	3.02	3.73	3.1	3.99	4.17	4.45	4.6	3.46	3.45	2.9
South Carolina	3.37	4.52	3.86	3.24	3.70	5.26	5.74	5.31	3.82	3.17	2.40
South Dakota	0.57	0.91	1.56	1.09	3.65	4.4	2.79	3.49	1.62	1.4	0.37
Tennessee	4.90	4.19	6.87	4.06	3.91	4.26	4.61	3.65	3.04	2.56	4.08
Texas	1.48	1.80	2.02	2.79	3.85	3.27	3.12	2.37	2.76	2.62	2.37
Virginia	3.13	3.49	4.09	3.28	4.05	4.31	4.7	4.53	3.49	3.23	2.59
Washington	4.98	4.55	3.33	2.44	2.48	1.86	0.76	0.82	2.12	2.83	5.89
West Virginia	3.47	3.06	4.10	3.50	4.28	4.57	4.86	4.12	2.66	2.4	2.97
Wisconsin	1.23	1.19	2.04	2.20	3.84	4.02	4.06	3.12	3.22	2.56	1.70

Cotton.

Cotton is one of the greatest factors in our export trade and is growing in importance from year to year. In 1901 cotton made up, in dollars, about 18% of our total exports of merchandise; in 1903, 22%; in 1905, 25%; in 1907, 27%; in 1909, 27%, and in 1910, 29%. This was partly due to larger exports and partly to higher prices.

The condition, acreage and production of cotton in the growing season for a period of years has been as follows:

Condition of Cotton in Growing Season on the First of Month Named.

Period 1901 to 1911 Inclusive.

Year	June	July	Aug.	Sept.	Oct.
1901......	81.5	81.1	77.2	71.4	61.4
1902......	95.1	84.7	81.9	64.0	58.3
1903......	74.1	77.1	79.7	81.2	65.1
1904......	83.0	88.0	91.6	84.1	75.8
1905......	77.2	77.0	74.9	72.1	71.2
1906......	84.6	83.3	82.9	77.3	71.6
1907......	70.5	72.0	75.0	72.7	67.7
1908......	79.7	81.2	83.0	76.1	69.7
1909......	81.1	74.6	71.9	63.7	58.5
1910......	82.0	87.0	63.7	72.1	65.9
1911......	87.8	88.2	89.1	73.2	71.1

Acreage and Production of Cotton 1901 to 1911 Inclusive.

(Production in bales 500 pounds to the bale.)

Years	Acreage	Production
1901-2..........	27,950,000	9,675,771
1902-3..........	27,874,000	10,827,168

Years	Acreage	Production
1903-4..........	28,907,000	10,045,615
1904-5..........	31,730,000	13,679,954
1905-6..........	26,117,000	10,804,556
1906-7..........	31,347,000	13,595,498
1907-8..........	31,311,000	11,375,461
1908-9..........	32,444,000	13,587,306
1909-10.........	31,918,000	10,290,395
1910-11.........	33,196,000	11,426,000
1911-12.........	35,000,000	16,050,000

In the above tables the progress of the crop in August is represented by the condition figures of September 1, etc. In the table of acreage and production, the years are separated as they are because the picking of cotton is not completed or the total crop known until the following year. In comparing the condition and production figures, the last figure in "years" may be disregarded. Thus condition of 1904 applies to production of 1904-5, etc.

It will be observed that either a high or low condition of cotton in the early months frequently ends in a disappointing crop. This is more pronounced in cotton than in cereals. Only twice in twenty years have we had a June condition above 90 (1896, 97.2; 1902, 95.1) and on both occasions the crop was a failure. In 1896 the condition fell from 92.5 on July 1 to 64.2 on September 1, and 60.7 on October 1. In 1902 the final condition was 58.3. On the other hand, a low June condition frequently ends in a good crop, as may be seen by reference to the foregoing tables. August is usually the crucial month. While it is well to keep track of acreage and condition in the early months, the daily study of weather and precipitation during the latter part of July and the entire month of August will give us our first dependable line on probable production.

The cotton producing states are given below in the order of their importance.

Cotton Producing States and Yield of 1910.

(In bales, 500 pounds to the bale.)

State	Yield 1910 (bales)
Texas	3,140,000
Georgia	1,750,000
Alabama	1,174,000
Mississippi	1,160,000
South Carolina	1,116,000
Oklahoma	900,000
Arkansas	815,000
North Carolina	675,000
Tennessee	305,000
Louisiana	260,000
Florida	58,000
Missouri	48,000
Virginia	13,000
California	12,000
Total	11,426,000

Cotton is more subject to damage by frost than is any other important crop. This is because the plant is more or less perennial. That is to say, it continues to put out new bolls late into the fall, until stopped by frost. The following table shows the date of the first killing frost in the principal cotton growing states for a period of years.

Date of First Killing Frost.

	Season of 1909-10	Season of 1908-09	Season of 1907-08	Season of 1906-07	Season of 1905-06
North Carolina ..Charlotte	Oct. 25	Nov. 15	Nov. 14	Oct. 12	Nov. 11
" Rockingham	Oct. 17	Nov. 5	Nov. 28	Oct. 11	Nov. 12
" Raleigh	Oct. 30	Nov. 5	Oct. 22	Oct. 12	Nov. 15
" Goldsboro	Oct. 26	Nov. 7	Oct. 22	Oct. 12	Nov. 12
South Carolina ..Charleston	Dec. 10	None	Nov. 14	Nov. 16	Dec. 11
" Columbia	Nov. 19	Nov. 6	Oct. 29	Oct. 29	Nov. 22
Georgia ....Atlanta	Oct. 25	Nov. 6	Oct. 14	Oct. 11	Oct. 22
" Augusta	Nov. 19	Nov. 15	Nov. 14	Oct. 29	Nov. 12
" Savannah	Dec. 10	Dec. 9	Nov. 14	Nov. 13	Dec. 4
" Columbus	Oct. 25	Nov. 15	Nov. 13	Nov. 13	Nov. 23
" Rome	Oct. 25	Nov. 6	Oct. 14	Oct. 11	Oct. 22
Florida ....Jacksonville	Dec. 10	None	Dec. 5	Nov. 13	None
" Pensacola	Dec. 21	None	Dec. 5	Dec. 23	Dec. 5
Alabama ....Eufaula	Oct. 25	Nov. 15	Nov. 14	Oct. 29	Nov. 23
" Mobile	Dec. 21	None	None	Dec. 24	Dec. 4
" Montgomery	Nov. 19	Nov. 15	Nov. 13	Nov. 13	Nov. 30
Mississippi ...Vicksburg	Nov. 18	Nov. 12	Nov. 13	Nov. 13	Nov. 30
" Greenville	Oct. 25	Oct. 29	Oct. 14	Oct. 11	Nov. 2

Date of First Killing Frost (Continued)

		Season of 1909-10	Season of 1908-09	Season of 1907-08	Season of 1906-07	Season of 1905-06
Louisiana	......New Orleans	Dec. 21	None	None	Dec. 24	Dec. 5
"	......Shreveport	Nov. 18	Nov. 14	Nov. 12	Nov. 1	Nov. 30
Texas	.........Galveston	None	None	None	None	None
"	.........Palestine	Dec. 8	Nov. 14	Nov. 12	Nov. 22	Dec. 3
"	.........San Antonio	Dec. 9	Nov. 14	Nov. 13	Nov. 20	Dec. 4
"	.........Fort Worth	Nov. 18	Nov. 13	Nov. 11	Nov. 1	Nov. 29
Arkansas	......Little Rock	Nov. 18	Nov. 12	Nov. 12	Nov. 22	Nov. 30
"	......Fort Smith	Nov. 17	Nov. 12	Nov. 11	Oct. 31	Nov. 29
Tennessee	......Memphis	Nov. 17	Nov. 12	Nov. 11	Nov. 13	Nov. 30
"	......Nashville	Oct. 13	Nov. 6	Oct. 29	Oct. 11	Oct. 22
"	......Chattanooga	Oct. 25	Nov. 6	Nov. 13	Oct. 11	Nov. 12
Oklahoma	......Ardmore	Nov. 17	Oct. 24	Nov. 10	Oct. 31	Oct. 21
"	......Oklahoma City ..	Nov. 17	Oct. 24	Nov. 12	Oct. 30	Oct. 20
"	......Mangum	Nov. 16	Oct. 24	Nov. 12	Nov. 12	Oct. 20

The two last tables give the latest statistics available. That they are not up to date is of little importance as we may determine from the exhibits about what are normal conditions.

CHAPTER IV.

Security Prices and Crop Prospects.

While the crucial period for our leading cereal crops, as to their effect on security prces, is during the months of July, August and September, it is necessary for us to keep a constant watch on progress during the months of April, May and June, in order to keep fully informed as to soil conditions, acreage, etc.

As has been stated, the period from July 1 to September 1, is the one in which crop prospects are the dominant factor. If investigations are prop- the dominant factor. If investigations are properly conducted, the greatest opportunities of the year, together with the largest amount of material on which to base conclusions, is offered during these three months. There is a hazy popular idea that June, July and August are vacation months and that comparatively narrow movements occur during this period. But not so. August is the most active month of the entire year and the month in which greatest general advances are shown. This is not always reflected in volume of security transactions, but it is evident in price changes. August has been a month of advancing prices in all but three recent years. This is due to the fact that crop prospects are pretty well known by August 1, and if damage has occurred it has already been discounted in security prices. It would not do at all to merely accept the fact that August has almost always been a "bull" month in the past, and operate blindly on that principle. That would be chart playing pure and simple. But if we take the trouble to examine crop prospects

carefully, to determine how much damage has
been done and whether or not the damage has
been discounted in security prices, adding to this
a general survey of business conditions and a
comparison of income yield on stocks as compared with the price of money, we have a simple
and very solid basis on which to operate. At
no other time of the year, will our indications
of probable price movements be so easily read as
in the three months of the crop growing period.

In order to show the dominance of crop prospects as a factor in the security market, the following tables and data have been prepared.

Table Showing Total Cereal and Cotton Production 1897 to 1910, Inclusive

(Cereals used are Wheat, Corn, Oats, Oats, Rye and Barley.)

	Total Cereal Production (Bushels)	Total Cotton Production (Bales)
1897	3,225,933,000	10,989,052
1898	3,411,689,000	11,534,303
1899	3,517,487,000	9,459,935
1900	3,519,879,000	10,266,527
1901	3,157,056,000	9,675,771
1902	4,350,138,000	10,827,168
1903	3,827,315,000	10,045,615
1904	4,081,459,000	13,679,954
1905	4,518,456,000	10,804,556
1906	4,839,872,000	13,595,498
1907	4,166,013,000	11,375,461
1908	4,339,016,000	13,587,306
1909	4,719,441,000	10,290,395
1910	5,143,187,000	11,426,000

Table showing the movements of security prices in June, July and August, 1897 to 1910, inclusive:

(Average advance or decline in points, "Wall Street Journal's" figures.)

	June		July		August		June 1 to August 31	
	Adv.	Dec.	Adv.	Dec.	Adv.	Dec.	Adv.	Dec.
1897	3.60	....	3.01	....	5.37	....	11.98	....
1898	....	1.39	.51	....	2.59	....	1.71	....
1899	5.89	....	1.30	....	.41	....	7.60	....
1900	....	5.49	.67	....	.80	....	....	4.02
1901	2.63	....	....	7.96	3.80	....	....	1.53
1902	1.19	....	5.18	....	1.45	....	7.82	....
1903	.32	....	....	7.51	1.68	....	....	5.51
1904	2.99	....	2.98	....	4.02	....	9.99	....
1905	5.57	....	2.90	....	3.94	....	12.41	....
1906	....	5.51	7.35	....	4.75	....	6.59	....
1907	4.64	....	.46	....	....	7.03	....	1.95
1908	....	2.17	6.84	....	2.20	....	6.87	....
1909	2.04	....	3.68	....	....	.80	4.92	....
1910	....	6.69	....	2.96	3.72	....	....	5.93
1911	1.12	....	0.27	....	....	8.01	....	6.62

Taking up the years seriatim, we find the following facts:

1897.—Very large crops—Wheat and cotton broke all previous records. Prospects excellent in June, July and August. Stock market made great advance.

1898.—The June decline followed a very rapid advance of over ten points in May. In this year, we again broke all previous records for wheat and cotton. After September the market continued rapidly upward until the end of the year.

1899.—Combined production of wheat, corn and oats was larger than in 1898, and the June prospects were excellent. Cotton, however, fell off 2,000,000 bales as compared with the preceding year, and final production of wheat was smaller by about 130,000,000 bushels. The reason for the June enthusiasm was due to good initial crop prospects which dwindled rapidly. The early condition of winter wheat was given as 77.9, but at harvest was 65.6. June condition of spring wheat was 91.4, and August condition 83.6. June cotton condition was 85.7 and at harvest 62.4. Corn and oats made large yields and the June advances in security prices was maintained, but did not continue rapidly.

1900.—Total cereal production exceeded that of the preceding year by only a narrow margin and wheat production again fell off—25,000,000 bushels less than 1899 and over 150,000,000 less than 1898. Cotton was a fair crop, but this was not indicated in the early reports, June 1 condition being 82.5 and July 1. 75.8. During the month of June the condition of spring wheat dropped from 87.3 on the first of the month to 55.2 at the end of the month. This terrific slump in prospects was the greatest specific cause of the June break.

1901.—We started off with excellent crop prospects in June and finally made the largest wheat crop in history. But in July it became apparent that a great falling off would occur in corn and oats. Later, cotton prospects became poorer. The July break was the most severe shown in any declining month in the period considered, and a glance at the total cereal production given in the table above will show that these fears were well based and accurately reflected in security prices. The greatest damage was to corn. So severe was the drought of 1901, that prayers for rain were offered in many Western states by official proclamation of the governors. One peculiarity of this scare in 1901, was that for some reason the Government greatly erred in their calculations of total cereal yield. The first figures given for wheat, corn, oats, rye and barley, by the Department of Agriculture were 2,791,346,000 bushels, and the census figures issued later gave 3,157,066,000 bushels.

1902.—In 1902 we broke all records for cereal production. Wheat production was smaller than the revised figures of 1901, but corn was greater by more than one billion bushels, and the cotton crop was the largest on record, with the exception of 1898. This was all reflected in the stock market.

1903.—This was one of our panic years, and in July, we had a hard time with the elements. In the West, tremendous damage occurred from excessive rainfall and floods; in the East, we suffered from extensive forest fires in the Adirondacks. The floods caused great damage to railroads and to farm work. Damage to crops was considerably over-estimated, particularly the flood damage, and while cereal production fell off, the decrease was nothing like what was expected in July. Cotton also turned out better than expected.

1904.—The same argument may be adduced here as was the case in 1897—i. e., that we were recovering from a period of depression. But, as in the former case, that recovery had gone a long way before crop prospects became a market factor. Cereal production was not so large as in 1902, but was larger than in any preceding year with that exception. The cotton crop was the largest ever made either before that year or since, the current crop excepted.

1905.—All records for cereal production were broken. Cotton was a fair crop by comparison with all preceding years except 1904. It is a strange fact that the most sensational attempts at crop killing for years were made in July. Wheat advanced 7 cents a bushel between July 18 and July 21 on talk of drouth and black rust. The damage was, in truth, comparatively nothing. This was also the month of the scandal in the cotton bureau which resulted in the resignation of the chief statistician. The juggling of the cotton report resulted in issuing figures which carried cotton up 100 points in a few minutes. These figures were afterwards revised by the Government. The crop scares were so obviously wrong, that they were refuted by well posted people, and only a moderate decline occurred, which was quickly recovered.

1906.—June of this year was filled with political scares. Congress was in session until the end of the month. The Hepburn rate bill became a law, President Roosevelt transmitted several reports to Congress which were considered inimical to corporate enterprise, and the pure food bill became a law. There was some apprehension about crops which was largely due to the June Government report on winter wheat, showing a falling off of over 6 points as compared with the preceding year. The Government again badly underestimated one of our leading cereal crops, indicating that oats would fall off about 150,000,000 bushels as compared with 1905. The crop turned out larger than 1905. The acreage devoted to oats was underestimated by about 3,000,000 acres.

After the July flurry, crop prospects steadily improved and total cereal production again made a record. The cotton crop was very large, almost equalling the high figures of 1904.

1907.—Another panic year, but crop prospects had some market effect. Condition of winter and spring wheat was satisfactory early in the season, but both crops went backward considerably before harvest. Cotton condition was low in June. After the Government reports of June 10, the crop news improved throughout the month, but this news was not borne out by the Government reports of July 10. The total cereal crop fell off sharply as compared with both 1905 and 1906.

The cotton crop was a good one except by comparison with the very large years 1904 and 1906. Crops did not dominate movements in this particular year so much as is usually the case, as money conditions were causing great confusion and irregularity. The August decline does not appear to be justified by crop prospects. It was in August, 1907, that the State of Alabama revoked the charter of the Southern Pacific to do business in Alabama, and close on the heels of this came the hysterical $29,000,000 Standard Oil fine. The State of Arkansas attempted to declare forfeited the property of the Rock Island road in that state, and numerous other state measures were agitated. This added to an already over-strained condition of affairs, and it is doubtful if even the most glowing crop prospects could have done more than cancel a portion of the decline.

1908.—Cereal production turned out well in 1908 and we made another bumper crop of cotton. The June decline in security prices followed a rapid advance of 16 points on the average in April and May, and may be considered as partly due to reaction. The progress of the cotton crop was the principal incentive to prices, the July 1 report of condition of 83 on August 1 was the highest in that month for ten years with one exception (1904).

1909.—Cereal production largest on record, with one exception. The season started with glowing prospects, but later on cotton reports showed up badly, condition falling 17 points between June 1 and September 1. This stopped the advance promptly.

1910.—Cereal production in 1910 turned out very satisfactorily, the total yield being the largest on record. The June decline was largely due to very bad conditions in spring wheat. The report of July 1 showed a condition of 61.6 as compared with 92.8 on June 1. Cotton was also acting badly, condition falling from 82.0 on June 1 to 63.7 on August 1. This was a double blow, but in the middle of July it was figured that in spite of the bad conditions, our general cereal crop would be the largest on record and that cotton would make a fair crop. The market began recovering and advanced until September.

It is clear from the above that the three-month period from June 1 to September 1 is one in which crop prospects make the market. It is also shown that while this period offers some of the greatest speculative opportunities, we can never be sure we are out of the woods before August 1 at the earliest. June has been the month of greatest uncertainty, as advances or declines in that month are more nearly equal in number. July shows a large majority of advances simply because crop prospects have been good in a majority of years. July breaks, when they do come, are rather severe. August shows only one insignificant decline, aside from the break of 1907, which, as has been explained, was not due to crop prospects. The reason for the large number of advances in August can be attributed to the fact that by that time prospects are pretty satisfactorily determined, and damage, if severe, has already been discounted in security prices.

CHAPTER V.

Money.

Much benefit may be derived from the study of money conditions. At times indications in this quarter are so plainly evident that they cannot be misunderstood, and it is remarkable that such signals are frequently disregarded or their purport misinterpreted or contorted. In the latter part of 1906 and early in 1907 the expansion of credits was so serious that even a perfunctory knowledge of the functions of money and credits should have shown the danger of panic conditions in the very near future. We were trying to finance a business boom and a stock market boom simultaneously, and it could not be done. One or the other had to suffer at once, and the lot fell to the stock market. The great decline in stocks in 1907 was partly due to the fact that the stock market had fully discounted the prosperity of 1907 and had begun discounting a period of depression; but the fact that the market underwent a spasm of demoralization instead of an orderly readjustment of prices was largely due to our expansion of credits.

The best barometer of contraction or expansion of credits is the percentage of loans to deposits; but the percentage of specie to loans should be considered in connection with loans and deposits, as a high percentage of loans to deposits might not be serious if the percentage of specie to loans is also high, and vice versa. It is when the two spread apart; when loans are high and specie low, that the greatest danger exists. It is not always the case that a very low percentage of loans to deposits, accompanied by a high percentage of specie, is encouraging. This condition may arise from stagnation, as was the case in 1894 and 1895.

During the last ten years we have witnessed two stock market panics, one in 1903 and one in 1907. Both were indicated by a high condition of loans to deposits and a low condition of specie to loans. In the early part of 1903 loans reached 102% of deposits. This was the first time loans had exceeded deposits since 1896. Specie simultaneously fell below 18% of loans. The stock market suffered a serious decline. In August, 1904, this condition was fully corrected, loans to deposits falling to 91% and specie to loans rising to about 25½%. A great upward movement followed in the stock market. In July, 1906, loans began expanding and reached about 107% in December of that year, specie falling at the same time to 17% of loans. The decline of 1907 followed. This condition was rapidly corrected in 1908, and by April of that year loans to deposits were below 96 and specie to loans above 26. The stock market advanced rapidly. We may find the same parallel for many years back, both as regards the great swings of prices and the smaller intermediate swings. In consulting such records, however, due allowance must be made for even worse conditions near the end of a panic than at its beginning. In December, 1903, loans to deposits rose to almost 105%, with specie to loans down to 18%, and in November, 1907, loans to deposits rose to 110%, while specie dropped below 15%. This bad state of affairs had already been discounted in security prices and was not due to over-expansion of credits, but to the hoarding of money and general lack of confidence. It was the final spasm of a panic period. It is the initial and insidious growth before the decline that must be watched for danger signals, not the final convulsion. In the early stages, the high rate of loans represents over-confidence, wildcat enterprises and extravagance; in the latter stages, nothing but temporary fright.

In consulting the figures of percentage of loans to deposits some allowance must be made for the growing loanable surplus of banks, particularly as the associated banks of New York furnish our only convenient barometer from week to week. This is not a great factor, however. It is also occasionally the case that better or worse conditions obtain in the west than in New York. An examination of the occasional calls of the Comptroller will keep us reasonably well posted on the condition of all national banks. It is found that the uniformity is not often nor seriously disturbed, and the figures of the New York banks constitute a fairly accurate guide.

No cut and dried figures as to just what constitutes the proper percentage of loans to deposits or specie to loans can be given, but we may say, as a rough rule of thumb, that a percentage of loans to deposits of from 95 to 100, together with a percentage of specie to loans of 20 to 23, is a normal state of affairs. These figures will vary a little at times.

The tables which follow, showing percentage of specie to loans and loans to deposits for a period of years will be found convenient in examining this phase of money conditions.

TABLE SHOWING PERCENTAGE OF SPECIE TO LOANS FOR YEARS 1882 TO 1910.

	Jan.	Feb.	March	April	May	June	July	Aug.	Sept.	Oct.	Nov.	Dec.
1882	19.27	20.26	16.62	18.34	20.86	10.58	17.38	17.49	16.33	16.02	16.38	17.08
1883	18.94	19.47	16.90	16.28	17.67	19.60	19.11	19.33	18.40	17.36	16.18	17.84
1884	18.97	21.83	22.31	18.78	16.37	15.26	20.79	25.57	26.16	26.23	26.54	30.03
1885	29.50	35.77	34.33	34.51	37.58	38.33	37.14	37.70	35.19	32.38	27.52	27.05
1886	26.39	29.22	25.31	22.42	20.77	19.67	18.12	18.17	20.71	21.78	22.60	22.18
1887	24.54	26.01	23.08	21.33	21.03	19.85	20.16	20.77	19.88	21.79	21.88	19.23
1888	20.89	23.28	20.46	16.77	22.07	23.77	23.91	23.07	21.13	21.46	22.83	21.10
1889	19.66	22.30	20.88	18.43	19.91	17.56	17.27	17.71	18.79	16.52	18.37	19.04
1890	19.37	22.25	19.02	20.06	19.49	19.02	18.89	20.01	17.78	23.34	19.43	17.55
1891	20.40	22.33	19.40	18.68	17.76	15.47	16.82	17.61	14.67	15.81	19.93	21.49
1892	21.88	24.31	21.38	20.80	20.31	21.11	18.53	18.54	16.33	15.47	16.40	17.79
1893	17.36	17.95	15.97	16.52	16.48	16.84	15.22	13.68	16.71	21.45	24.14	25.49
1894	26.52	30.88	22.20	22.11	21.51	21.51	18.86	18.77	18.61	18.43	18.72	15.32
1895	15.38	16.63	14.37	13.42	14.38	14.05	12.16	12.85	12.43	11.94	12.82	12.94
1896	14.81	17.18	13.25	12.73	12.60	12.96	12.99	9.85	11.08	12.31	14.40	16.01
1897	15.54	15.99	16.94	17.10	17.26	17.44	16.98	16.76	16.23	16.15	17.80	17.48
1898	17.48	18.00	19.10	23.75	27.98	29.17	29.96	26.02	22.07	21.45	23.19	22.71
1899	24.29	26.59	25.42	23.99	24.26	27.55	23.19	21.98	22.30	20.72	20.19	21.31
1900	21.24	23.27	20.95	20.08	21.00	21.27	20.59	21.97	21.65	20.00	19.94	20.74
1901	20.52	22.11	21.24	20.22	20.47	20.91	19.09	20.55	19.22	20.64	20.01	19.23
1902	18.95	21.67	20.56	19.09	19.22	19.47	19.00	18.86	17.83	17.34	19.86	18.38
1903	17.70	19.24	17.95	17.49	18.31	17.12	17.36	18.78	18.68	18.34	17.71	17.18
1904	17.67	20.62	21.92	21.85	21.53	21.87	22.26	24.94	24.28	21.37	20.30	19.50
1905	19.05	20.15	19.36	19.06	20.17	18.57	19.17	10.38	18.81	18.41	18.00	17.57
1906	16.66	18.30	17.56	16.64	17.53	17.42	17.26	18.15	17.09	18.25	17.83	17.33
1907	16.49	18.03	17.42	19.48	18.67	19.48	17.91	18.68	18.41	17.66	15.32	14.66

TABLE SHOWING PERCENTAGE OF LOANS TO DEPOSITS FOR YEARS 1882 TO 1910.

	Jan.	Feb.	March	April	May	June	July	Aug.	Sept.	Oct.	Nov.	Dec.
1882	106.54	103.98	110.36	109.88	104.17	106.62	105.76	104.78	107.59	109.92	110.12	109.41
1883	104.82	103.04	106.94	110.39	106.26	102.14	101.97	100.99	103.22	104.50	105.29	102.76
1884	100.44	95.44	96.03	101.08	102.63	106.81	100.78	94.69	95.02	94.22	92.34	87.33
1885	87.40	83.14	85.49	85.86	82.78	81.35	80.69	79.90	83.12	85.84	89.56	89.91
1886	90.18	86.91	90.16	94.34	90.23	94.10	94.26	95.03	98.00	98.12	97.23	97.21
1887	94.15	92.49	95.93	98.12	99.40	98.36	99.05	99.44	100.13	99.08	98.23	100.25
1888	96.98	94.20	97.36	99.15	95.31	92.91	91.98	92.17	95.00	95.80	94.43	95.99
1889	95.90	92.70	94.24	97.46	94.83	95.25	94.90	95.00	95.82	98.87	98.54	98.96
1890	97.54	94.45	100.29	99.11	98.47	97.70	97.65	96.53	101.73	97.24	100.94	102.53
1891	99.72	95.50	98.13	99.30	99.30	100.63	97.34	96.12	99.41	100.83	98.64	96.36
1892	94.04	89.46	91.64	92.60	92.92	90.97	92.40	92.51	95.61	97.52	98.55	99.93
1893	96.93	93.80	98.01	98.79	97.65	96.58	103.95	109.33	106.90	98.30	89.91	84.05
1894	80.70	76.01	82.64	81.27	80.40	81.25	82.14	82.97	83.68	84.87	84.10	86.18
1895	89.27	89.62	91.64	95.95	92.06	88.74	91.17	88.78	89.83	94.47	94.51	93.94
1896	94.74	91.12	95.09	96.50	95.11	95.93	95.41	96.87	101.30	99.60	100.80	94.10
1897	92.55	87.40	86.93	88.31	87.60	88.02	88.03	87.76	88.75	92.36	90.89	89.71
1898	88.91	86.30	88.92	87.32	86.52	84.86	82.79	85.81	89.30	90.51	88.29	88.33
1899	86.33	84.23	85.30	86.73	86.33	83.89	86.93	88.69	88.78	90.91	92.01	91.21
1900	90.50	87.91	90.90	91.89	90.63	90.12	91.04	89.80	90.42	93.10	93.59	93.00
1901	92.44	89.98	90.33	91.76	91.53	90.97	92.15	91.91	93.41	92.58	93.10	93.89
1902	93.88	91.15	92.25	94.05	93.39	93.49	95.02	96.00	98.24	100.02	98.30	100.19
1903	100.25	98.38	100.31	101.72	100.92	101.84	101.51	99.89	100.70	101.75	103.69	104.63
1904	102.53	97.25	96.14	93.91	94.69	94.40	93.32	90.98	91.80	92.03	95.30	96.77
1905	96.46	92.73	95.41	96.57	95.54	96.94	96.13	95.75	97.50	100.06	100.59	101.67
1906	102.13	99.09	101.15	102.96	101.47	101.50	101.40	100.11	102.08	102.07	103.72	105.00
1907	104.96	102.03	103.00	102.57	101.81	101.05	103.50	102.54	104.72	105.12	109.27	110.46
1908	104.83	99.89	98.63	96.47	94.02	93.81	94.01	90.98	92.96	94.46	94.37	95.89
1909	94.94	96.18	96.63	96.67	95.86	94.98	94.64	95.98	97.90	99.80	101.28	101.85
1910	101.61	98.53	99.41	100.12	101.98	100.81	100.62	98.71	97.93	100.69	103.28	102.50

The seasonal movements of money are natural and inevitable and interest rates may rise or fall in certain months without materially disturbing the course of the security markets. Interest rates usually begin rising early in December, and continue to rise during the first week or ten days in January. This is principally due to preparation for the large January disbursements in the form of interest on bonds and notes and dividends on stocks. The holiday trade is also a factor. After the first week or ten days of January, the funds which have been distributed begin to be redeposited or reinvested, and money becomes more plentiful. Interest rates ordinarily fall until the end of January and remain low until the middle of February, when the demand for funds in preparation for the spring trade again causes rates to harden. April, May and June are usually months of declining interest rates, but near the middle of June large fiscal institutions begin providing for the July disbursements. This causes an upward trend in interest rates. There is, however, no following decline as is the case after the January rise. This is due to the fact that the crop moving period is at hand and the demand for money will be greater for several months to come than at any time during the year. Near the middle of August funds begin to flow westward and are fully employed until the end of October. The highest prices for money ordinarily occur in October, after which there is a slow decline until the preparations for the January disbursements of the following year bring a hardening of rates.

It is found that in a majority of cases there has been an advance in the stock market during December and January. This advance has usually started near the middle of December and culminated early in February. This represents the forehanded buying by speculators who anticipate and discount the return flow of funds into the security markets in January. There is also, in a majority of cases, an advance in the stock market in the latter part of July and throughout the month of August. This upward movement, simultaneously with advancing money rates, is due to crop prospects which are pretty well known in August and which are much more frequently favorable than unfavorable. The month of September shows a decline in stock prices in most cases, as the crops are then no longer in much doubt and the favorable effects have been fully discounted. The incentive to buy on good crop prospects has been great enough in August to overcome the advancing trend of money rates, but the acute stages in money begin in September and this influence makes itself apparent.

It would be ridiculous to assume that a safe mechanical plan for buying and selling in certain seasons can be formulated. Nevertheless the price of money always has its effect on speculative operations, and it is essential that we know what is natural in different periods of the year, so that we may not be deterred from operations because of a misunderstanding of the seasonal changes. It is frequently the case that people who are satisfied with business or crop prospects become alarmed at rapidly advancing prices for money and abandon their plans. Their fears are increased by the warnings of writers or prophets who either **do not** know what they are talking about or are interested in promulgating fallacious views.

In considering the effect of money rates on speculative investments we will also find it wise to give attention to the occasional hiatus between call and time funds. During most of the year the prices of call and time money rise and fall together, but July and August are ordinarily exceptions to this rule. In July, particularly,we find a declining trend in call money in the face of an advancing trend in commercial paper because, while the banks are storing up funds for the drain in the crop moving period, they can employ such funds from day to day and still hold them available by loaning on call. This affects only the larger speculators, as most brokerage houses have a rate of interest to clients which remains practically unchanged the year round. However, the advantage gained by the large operators encourages them to make ventures, and the general market is helped accordingly.

One of the simplest and most reliable methods of determining when the general average of security prices is too high or too low is to measure the average yield, at the market price, on seasoned dividend payers, and compare that yield with the price of money. It is shown that in the last ten years the lowest average yield on ten selected dividend paying railroad stocks was slightly over 3% in the latter part of 1906 and the highest yield on the same stocks for the same period of years was 7¼% in November, 1907. In other words, the prices of these securities went so high in 1906 that the return on money invested at the market price would only be about 3% and so low in 1907 that they returned over 7% on the market price.   Looking backward now it is very easy to see that in one case prices were ridiculously high, and in the other ridiculously low; but how many people took advantage of such knowledge? They were carried away by the speculative debauch late in 1906 and were unduly repressed and apprehensive in the panic period late in 1907. In the latter part of 1906, when these stocks were yielding only 3%, time money ruled steadily at 6% or above.   True, in 1907, time money got as high as 8% while the stocks were returning 7%, but everyone knew, or should have known, that such rates were only temporary.   In January, 1908, time money was down to $5\frac{1}{4}$%, and in May, 1908, $3\frac{1}{2}$%.

The yield on a specific stock may at times appear unduly low and at the same time the stock may be a good purchase, because of forthcoming rights or extra distributions or because of the probability of an increase in the dividend rate.   All these things must be considered, but when the *average* rate of return rises above or falls below the fair value of money, a readjustment is inevitable.   Money will go where it can get the highest wages.

As in many other cases which confront us in forecasting security prices, no fixed rule as to when stocks are too low or too high as compared with money can be offered.   The value of money not only fluctuates considerably, but there is, sometimes, a definite trend to higher or lower interest rates over a period of years. Under existing circumstances, we may reasonably adopt the rough rule that when seasoned stocks with a good dividend record yield materially more than 5% they are cheap; and when they yield materially less than 5% they are dear.

After each period of panic or depression, when money begins to come back into the security markets and prices begin rising, we find a period of rotation. The bond and note markets first show strength and activity, then preferred stocks and high grade dividend payers are taken up, and finally the more speculative issues have their turn. In the final stages of a bull market, when speculation is rampant and inflation is present, there is not much discrimination; the excited public buys the wildcats as freely as it does the seasoned issues; more freely at times, for they present more golden opportunities to the imaginative buyer.

The observer of the first stages of a bull period will frequently find his views disturbed by writers who will admit that in all former periods an advance in the general market has been preceded by activity in bonds and high grade stocks; but, say these writers, "the conditions are different now. Money is going into high grade securities because the owners of money have no confidence in the general run of stocks." This argument is inevitable at the beginning of every period of rehabilitation. It appears extraordinary that any thinking man should consider it seriously. What the writers say is true as far as it goes but it does not go far. The reason which they give for the precedence of a certain class of securities has *always* been the reason for such precedence. Timidity is a personal characteristic of money, if the term is permissible. When money is sober, it is always cautious and discriminative; it is only when it is intoxicated that it becomes foolishly bold.

The state of our foreign credits is an elusive factor in money, and no statistics are obtainable on the subject. We may, however, make a fair estimate of our credits and the growth of credits abroad by watching exports and imports of merchandise and gold and other factors affecting our balances.

Our currency system is unquestionably a poor one, and many corrective suggestions have been offered, but none of them appear to solve the problem. In the following chapter Mr. C. F. McElroy has offered a plan which appears feasible, and which is worthy of serious consideration.

CHAPTER VI.

Relation of Inflexible Reserve Requirements to the Currency Question.

By C. F. McElroy.

Seasonal Stringency.

Of all the phenomena peculiar to the money market, the most remarkable is the wide fluctuation in interest rates in the New York market, due to the wide variations in the supply of loanable funds. These fluctuations are widest in the call loan market, but they are also in evidence in the time money market, although in a lesser degree. The recurrence of high rates is so regular that, by taking into consideration the state of general business throughout the country, farm production, etc., one may predict with a reasonable degree of certainty what course interest rates will take at any given period of the year, particularly as regards the last half of the year. In order to show these changes at a glance, I have taken the high and low rates for call money and four months' loans for the past twenty years, and averaged each month separately and brought the result together in the following table:

In examining these changes, it will be observed that, in the call money market, the average fluctuations in *any* month are quite wide, due to local causes; but it will also be observed that the tendency is toward a higher level during the last four months of the year. The tendency is not quite so marked in the time money market, but it is there. It should

AVERAGE HIGH AND LOW MONEY RATES
ON CALL AND FOUR MONTHS.

	On call	Four months
January	1½@13½%	3¾@ 4¾%
February	1½@ 3½	3⅝@ 4⅜
March	1½@ 7½	3¾@ 4⅝
April	1¾@ 6½	3⅝@ 4½
May	1½@ 8¾	3⅜@ 4⅜
June	1½@ 7½	3¼@ 4⅛
July	1¼@ 8¾	3⅝@ 4½
August	1½@ 6	4 @ 5
September	1½@ 8¼	4¼@ 5⅜
October	1¾@18½	4⅜@ 5¼
November	2 @17¼	4¼@ 5
December	2¼@30	4¼@ 5⅛

be stated in parenthesis, that in producing
these averages, some abnormally high rates
have had to be taken into the calculations; for
instance, in December, 1892, call rates reached
40%; December, 1895, 100%; December, 1899,
186%; December, 1905, 125%; November,
1896, 96%; November, 1907, 75%; October,
1896, 127%; October, 1907, 125%. It may be
argued that these abnormal instances unduly
raise the average and, therefore, should be
eliminated, but I think that a little reflection
will convince anyone that they should stay in,
as they form a part of the effects produced from
the causes which I shall attempt to make clear
in the course of this article.

The primary cause for the rise in interest
rates during the last four months of the year,
of course, is the demand for currency on the
part of the interior banks for the purpose of
moving the crops. This demand will be affected one way or the other by the varying state
of general business throughout the country.
If business is good, more currency will be
needed by the outside banks; if poor, less will

be needed. But, *always*, there are the crops, and they must be moved. The necessities for currency in that direction will also vary with the volume of farm production and the ruling level of prices, but they are always so large that they form one of the knottiest problems with which the New York banks have to deal.

Why, you ask, should this problem concern the New York banks in particular? It all arises from the attempt to impart some degree of elasticity to our currency system. The framers of the laws governing the reserves of national banks recognized the fact that, at certain periods of the year, country banks do not need to carry as large a reserve as at other periods, and that to compel them to do so would be a hardship. In other words, the demands for currency, which the reserve is intended to provide for, is less at times than it is at other times. They met the objection against country banks carrying reserves in cash equal at all times to a stated percentage of their deposits by giving them the privilege of carrying a portion of such reserves in the form of deposits with other designated "reserve" banks, and these "reserve" banks were, in addition, given the privilege of carrying a portion of their reserves in designated "central reserve" banks. The result is that, after the crops have been moved, the banks in the forty-seven "reserve" cities are flooded with cash, and they, in turn flood the "central reserve" cities, New York, Chicago and St. Louis. And a further result is that New York must find profitable employment for the bulk of this golden flood, for, obviously, it would not do to tie up very much of this sort of money in long time loans, and the market for call and other short time loans outside of New York being somewhat limited, Chicago and St. Louis banks compete with New York banks in the New York money market. When the crop-moving season arrives once more and the country banks begin to need currency, this money is withdrawn from New York, and New York banks are compelled to call in their demand and short time loans in order to keep their required reserves intact. Thus, while the system works admirably in imparting elasticity to the currency, so far as the country banks are concerned, it does not always work out so well for New York banks and their customers. In fact, more often than otherwise, in spite of all reasonable precautions, New York bankers are not always wholly prepared for this crop-moving demand when it arises; loans have to be called precipitately and gold imports resorted to, and when, as often happens, we are not in a position to import gold or are actually exporting it, the situation is greatly accentuated. Sometimes the Government assists by making deposits, but it is not always in a position to do that. Almost invariably between September 1 and the end of December, New York banks lose enormous sums of cash to the interior, and, in order to bring down their deposits proportionately with their diminished reserves, loans are called right and left. For the purpose of showing the extent of this movement of cash and its effect upon loans of the New York banks, the tables and chart on the pages following have been prepared:

CASH IN NEW YORK CLEARING HOUSE BANKS—EXTREME MOVEMENTS.

(In Millions of Dollars.)

	Jan.	Feb.	Mar.	Apr.	May.	June.	July.	Aug.	Sept.	Oct.	Nov.
1892	$132	$163	$149	$152	$148	$159	$151	$143	$124	$116	$119
1893	145	126	118	119	121	104	93	75	121	156	188
1894	245	249	208	221	227	217	217	212	207	211	214
1895	185	161	138	154	179	176	174	180	161	146	150
1896	159	146	137	142	146	146	141	123	125	128	153
1897	199	200	199	192	189	198	202	198	171	179	187
1898	216	205	204	208	226	246	226	210	182	216	208
1899	254	258	243	238	265	252	225	226	197	192	183
1900	223	231	205	229	237	241	249	252	252	213	224
1901	264	268	258	249	253	251	245	262	239	252	246
1902	261	266	245	242	241	251	253	243	220	238	244
1903	260	244	227	224	238	228	244	249	239	240	214
1904	280	288	289	311	288	323	357	360	328	313	293
1905	324	307	294	290	304	290	315	304	276	266	252
1906	246	276	256	248	266	274	283	267	246	275	248
1907	282	265	254	288	293	275	283	270	268	267	215
1908	318	325	337	371	383	367	396	414	401	385	379
1909	383	354	351	357	374	386	390	369	345	321	303
1910	343	333	319	305	322	329	307	371	339	308	300
1911	364	380	381	372	394	406	363	383	367	355	347
Avge	$254	$252	$240	$245	$254	$256	$255	$255	$240	$238	$233

LOANS OF NEW YORK CLEARING HOUSE BANKS—EXTREME MOVEMENTS.

(In Millions of Dollars.)

	Jan.	Feb.	Mar.	Apr.	May.	June.	July.	Aug.	Sept	Oct.	Nov.
1892	$438	$480	$494	$491	$488	$496	$480	$492	$475	$449	$442
1893	455	464	439	425	415	405	418	403	392	397	405
1894	419	441	445	460	467	470	483	488	497	500	495
1895	489	482	489	480	500	513	506	513	522	502	490
1896	447	462	467	467	475	474	479	455	450	446	442
1897	491	500	506	502	507	521	542	560	579	562	594
1898	625	646	600	570	589	612	639	672	642	635	693
1899	726	771	780	760	745	778	793	746	714	695	676
1900	688	745	763	774	792	810	797	817	825	793	785
1901	841	914	918	882	858	902	856	895	865	884	891
1902	869	936	938	893	870	893	913	929	874	865	879
1903	904	950	904	900	928	903	917	923	917	907	880
1904	994	999	1,007	1,049	1,078	1,036	1,099	1,099	1,140	1,145	1,102
1905	1,115	1,142	1,109	1,090	1,120	1,089	1,144	1,146	1,071	1,026	1,012
1906	1,041	1,061	1,019	1,009	1,049	1,060	1,036	1,077	1,036	1,082	1,039
1907	1,085	1,099	1,049	1,123	1,140	1,126	1,104	1,126	1,088	1,076	1,198
1908	1,117	1,161	1,164	1,195	1,219	1,239	1,270	1,290	1,322	1,338	1,347
1909	1,341	1,316	1,298	1,339	1,331	1,372	1,340	1,361	1,316	1,233	1,196
1910	1,218	1,232	1,245	1,251	1,183	1,199	1,208	1,248	1,281	1,226	1,201
1911	1,273	1,322	1,352	1,359	1,331	1,369	1,410	1,348	1,357	1,366	1,354
Avge	$828	$855	$849	$850	$854	$863	$871	$879	$868	$856	$856

CLEARING HOUSE BANKS, IN MILLIONS OF DOLLARS, AND AVERAGE

HIGH CALL MONEY RATES.

Solid Line, Loans; Dotted Line, Cash Holdings; Broken Line, Call Rates.

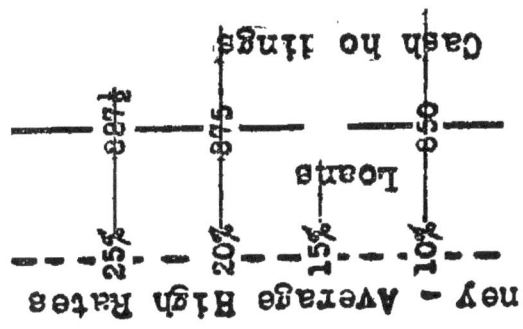

Cash no lings

Loans

ney — Average High Rates

$880

$875

$850

25%

20%

15%

10%

In the preparation of these tables, instead of averaging the four weeks of each month, the extreme of the diminishing or increasing trend, as the case may be, has been used in each instance, thus giving the full extent of each movement of currency into and out of the banks and the extreme high or low volume of loans. Each month has been averaged over the period of twenty years in order to give a composite view of the movements of currency and the accompanying expansion or reduction in loans, and these composite figures have been used in producing the chart which is presented as a convenient means of examining into what *usually* takes place. The exports and imports of gold, if taken into consideration, would accentuate rather than modify the lines which appear in the chart. They have, therefore, been left out of the calculations for the sake of simplicity.

Some of my readers, no doubt, will find fault because of the pains taken to establish the already well-known fact that New York is cursed with alternate periods of scarcity and plethora of loanable funds, but, outside of the ranks of those who make it their business to keep track of such things, there seems to be a great deal of confusion of ideas on the subject, and, as the preventative or corrective measure which will be proposed in the course of this chapter is of a somewhat revolutionary character, it was thought best to make the picture as clear and sharp as possible so that *all* may understand the *necessity* for some change in our system of money and credits.

The *necessity* for a change lies in the fact that, while the outlying districts are enabled, through the workings of our reserve laws, to increase or decrease their supply of currency at will—drawing down their deposits of currency with "reserve" banks when the exigencies of the crop-moving period or anticipation of greater business to follow in the wake of large crops demands more currency, or making their surplus funds earn something by depositing with "reserve" banks when the demands fo rcurrency fall off—the "reserve" centers in general and New York in particular must release cash just when it is most needed and receive cash when it is least needed. If the business of the country as a whole was not expanding each year, this state of affairs would be intolerable. As it is, the gradual expansion of bank loans from year to year absorbs the plethora, but something has to be sacrificed each year in order to take care of the scarcity. Each year a portion of the structure reared in the first half is torn down by the operations of the last half and must be rebuilt in the first half of the next year before the progress can be resumed.

Thus, while the balance of the country is provided with a neatly fitting circlet of elastic currency, New York banks are worse off than if there was absolute rigidity at that end. Their circlet is converted into a straight rubber band, with one end anchored in New York and the country pulling and hauling on the other end. Small wonder, then, that the tension frequently approaches the breaking point. A great many so-called remedies for this evil have been proposed. But all of them are cumbersome, and not easy to put in operation. Without exception, the plans offered are of such a complicated nature that even fairly well posted bankers find difficulty in following out their provisions, and, even when the plans are thoroughly understood, there is no certainty that their operation would bring the desired relief. I believe that a simple measure, which would bring relief for the greater part of our monetary troubles, has been found, and will endeavor to make it clear in the succeeding paragraphs.

Prevention of Autumnal Stringency.

Tons of printer's ink and paper have been used in the past to depict the bad effects of our present currency system. A lengthy discussion of that subject, therefore, would be a multiplication of words to no good purpose. The most effective argument so far produced has to do with the tendency of a plethora of loanable funds to promote over-speculation in securities, for the reason that New York banks, in order to protect themselves against a sudden call for currency by the interor banks, must make their loans against easily converted or liquid securities. This is undoubtedly true. When money is extremely cheap, speculators are tempted to borrow it in order to make the difference between the price of money and the yield on securities; and, when money becomes scarce and loans are being called, they must sell out at a loss or pay a high rate of interest to carry them through to the next period of cheap money. But it is not so much the woes of the speculators with which the financial community as a whole and the business interests of the country in general is concerned as it is with what sort of conditions would prevail if we had not this alternate ease and tightness with which to contend, although we cannot wholly ignore the claims of speculators to some consideration in the matter. Speculation, conducted within reasonable bounds, is a necessary adjunct to our economic development. Without it, the development of the natural resources of the country would not have advanced anywhere near so rapidly as it has. The speculation that is not of any benefit to the community and is harmful to it is that sort of crazy speculation which is induced by abnormally easy money rates plus misleading manipulation. If this periodical plethora of money in New York could be done away with, or at least modified to a considerable extent, much of this crazy speculation would be eliminated.

The simplest method of getting away from this congestion of funds in New York, the one which would rightfully receive the most condemnation, would consist of a change in the laws regulating the reserves of country banks. But such a change would be bitterly opposed by the country bankers for the simple reason that if they were not allowed to deposit a portion of their reserves with "reserve" banks, they would be deprived of a source of considerable revenue. And, furthermore, it would be opposed by banking interests generally for the reason that it would mean the tying up of vast sums in reserves which would be an economic waste of our financial resources. In short, it would mean that the plethora of money would simply be transferred from the New York group of banks to thousands of small country banks, and the flexibility of the currency, so far as the outlying districts are concerned, would be taken away without imparting any flexibility for New York. Obviously, any measure of this nature would be predoomed to failure.

It will be necessary, then, to devise a measure, if it is to receive the support of all concerned, that will not take away the privileges of the country banker or interfere with the flexibility of the currency outside of New York and which will impart flexibility to the currency of the *whole* country.

Now let us recapitulate a little and see how the flexibility of the currency in the interior has been accomplished. What causes the flexibility? The answer is obvious—the privilege enjoyed by the country banker of shipping out a big portion of the curency not actually needed, while still retaining the right to count such shipments (deposits with "reserve" banks) as a part of his own reserve against deposits in his own bank. In other words, the flexibility of the currency in the interior is accomplished by *flexibility of reserve requirements.* Simple and effective without doubt. It is the solution of the old problem of how to eat your cake and still have it.

But are the reserve requirements of the "central reserve" banks flexible? Not so. They must carry the required 25% or shut up shop. True, they are permitted by law to fall, temporarily, below 25% and are given 30 days' time in which to get back in line, but what bank or group of banks would dare to allow their reserves to drop below 25% for even a week with the law reading as it does. Confidence would receive an immediate jolt which would result in runs that would call for more reserves than any of the banks could muster. Nothing very much short of 100% would save them from the mob of besieging depositors. But, if the law regarding reserves read differently, confidence would be unimpaired so long as the banks observe the law.

The whole thing resolves itself into this—we have provided for flexibility in the currency through flexibility of reserve requirements in a great many small money centers and have not done so in a few great and important money centers. That is manifestly unjust; it is class legislation. Arguing from cause to effect and from effect back to cause again, it seems to me we ought to make this matter of flexible reserves a *reciprocal* affair. How is this to be accomplished?

Up to date, the answer has been, "Establish a Central Bank." That is easier said than done. A central bank for the United States, (not for the Government of the United States, but for the financial community of the United States), may be a solution or it may not be. I do not profess to know, and I venture to say that very few if any of the financial men of this country know with certainty that such an institution would actually accomplish what is needed. A great many think that it would, and are convinced in their own minds that it would, but there is so much complicated machinery connected with the workings of a central bank that those who understand it find it almost impossible to make others understand it. I believe that a central bank would relieve the "central reserve" banks of their present burdens to some extent, at least, but it would simply mean the transferring of the burden. If one institution strong enough to bear the burdens of the 59 "central reserve" banks, could be devised, it would be a grand thing. But there is where the element of doubt enters, and this element of doubt is one of the things which retards the progress of the movement to establish a central bank. Other countries have central banks which do the work satisfactorily, but those countries have passed through their periods of rapid growth. The one shining exception, of course, is Germany, and in that connection it is well to take note of the difficulties which have confronted the financial community of that country during the Franco-German crisis. They might have, and probably would have, been worse off if they had not been possessed of a central bank which, through its note issuing prerogative, undoubtedly proved of assistance in tiding over the crisis; but the existence of a central bank did not obviate the necessity for enforced liquidation in many quarters where the liquidation was detrimental to the rapid economic progress of the country. It is a little unfair, of course, to use the German central bank as an argument against a central bank in this country; as a matter of fact, I do not wish the reference to it to be construed as such. But, whether or not a central bank would do the work for which it is designed, the indications now are that we are a long way off from its establishment in this country.

The Corrective Measure.

Having no central bank to fall back upon, it seems to me that the simplest method of effecting a certain degree of flexibility for the *whole* country would be to allow the "central reserve" banks a little leeway in the matter of reserves at the time of greatest demand for currency. By reference to the tables already produced, it will be seen that, on the average, the time of greatest strain on the great money centers is during the months of September, October, November and December—the crop-moving period. Examination of the weekly reports of the New York clearing house banks shows that usually the drain of currency begins late in September and ends early in December. Why not so amend our banking laws that the "central reserve" banks, beginning on September 1 each year would be required to carry only 20% of their deposits in cash as a reserve, and during October and November, if necessary, only 15%, raising the requirements to 20% during December, restoring the reserve requirements to 25% during January and the succeeding months up to the following September. This would allow the "central reserve' banks to ship currency where needed without calling loans to bring their deposits down to the point where their cash reserves would equal 25% of the deposits.

If this were the law, and the intent of the law made so plain that every one would understand it as a measure designed to tide the whole country over a critical period which comes year after year at about the same time, no one would feel anxious or perturbed if the banks at the prescribed time allowed their reserves to fall below 25%. It would be an entirely different matter and be viewed by the public in a much different light than if a bank or a group of banks should unexpectedly take advantage of the 30-day leeway now permitted by law. The principle of the thing would be no different from that involved in the privilege enjoyed by the country banker who is allowed at *all times* to fall below 25% in actual cash in his vaults. Time has demonstrated that the principle is absolutely sound.

If this were the law, bankers in the "central reserve" cities would not be compelled to employ so much of the temporarily idle funds of the country in demand and other short time loans. They would put such funds out in longer time loans. which would mean greater stability in interest rates and greater permanency of the enterprises for which the money is borrowed, for the steady growth of the business of the country already creates a demand for these idle funds. But, as it is now, these idle funds are not as fully utilized in permanent investments as they should be. Bankers dare not allow loans to extend much beyond the critical month of September, and the economic development of the country is retarded thereby. We advance in a jerky movement, whereas the advancement should be steady and continuously in step with other basic economic factors. We would keep step financially with other things if bankers in the "central reserve" cities were not compelled during the last four months of the year to undo so much of the things accomplished during the first eight months.

Real Object of a Reserve.

When I first conceived the idea of imparting flexibility to the reserve requirements of the "central reserve" cities as a means of giving a certain degree of flexibility to the currency of the whole country, I confess that the idea seemed somewhat appalling. A 25% cash reserve for this class of banks has become such a sacred institution that it seemed nothing short of sacrilege to tamper with it. But, as I reflected upon it, it seemed to me that we have allowed ourselves to gain a wrong impression as to what the *real meaning of the word "reserve"* should be. Have we not set it up as a sort of a god to be gazed upon and worshipped, but not to be touched, even under the stress of most dire necessity? Why should we not look upon it as the business man or the corporation regards a reserve fund—as something which may be drawn against when the exigencies of business require it? A noted fiction writer, some years ago, added somewhat to his fame by means of a fanciful story about a big bank whose cash reserve of gold was surreptitiously replaced by pig iron and iron washers. The bank kept right on doing business, because the officials and, consequently, the public, had no slightest inkling of what had taken place, and the president of the bank, when the matter was brought to his attention by the perpetrator of the "experiment," was the most surprised man in the world over the preposterous idea that his bank could go on with its business without a dollar of reserve. The story was obviously overdrawn, but it contained a germ of truth, and that is that the prime essential in the banking business is *confidence.* Without confidence, a 25% reserve is as good as nothing. With confidence, 15% is as good as 100%, and better, because it allows of a greater employment of the bank's resources. Wherefore, the conclusion is forced upon me that if, at certain well determined periods of the year, we could facilitate the business of the country by an extension of banking facilities, then in the name of common sense let us extend them. And, if the extension can be accomplished by temporarily lowering reserve requirements, let us do that.

The main idea is in a crude state, and, no doubt, would have to be modified in a great many ways before it would find entire acceptance. For instance, there is the matter of security for the difference between 15% or 20% and the regular 25% reserve to be taken into consideration, but it seems to me that the banks would find little difficulty about putting up gilt-edged security equal to two, three or four times the amount of the temporary draft upon their cash reserves. There are, no doubt, many other objections which the trained bank manager could offer.

The measure is not submitted as a cure-all for our monetary ills; it is submitted as an expedient for bridging us over a definitely known and ever-recurring critical period—the crop-moving period.

Demonstration of the Measure.

The figures which follow have been produced for the purpose of showing what the effect would have been if this measure had been in force during the past twenty years.

In order to properly understand the figures which follow, a little preliminary explanation is necessary. But, first of all, it should be steadily kept in mind that there is a vast difference in the character of the demands for currency in the small money centers and that in the big centers like New York. In the small centers a large proportion of the currency wanted during the crop-moving period *is needed as currency* pure and simple; it circulates among the people. On the other hand, the currency is needed in New York, primarily, as *the basis of credit,* or, to put it another way, as reserves. It is in playing this dual role that our old favorite, "Hard Cash," frequently falls down. Every once in a while his lines call for his appearance on both sides of the stage at the same identical moment. If Shakespeare had found himself short of actors in producing the "Midsummer Night's Dream," I am sure he would have been resourceful enough to substitute something that would suggest a minor character, however remote the resemblance, just as he did with makeshifts for scenery, etc. We already have in circulation about all the makeshifts, in the way of Government bond secured currency, that is altogether safe. Further expansion in that direction would tend to drive the specie out of the country. Obviously, then, the problem is that of making what we have perform all functions with a minimum of friction, and, to that end, let us examine into credit conditions in New York as represented by bank loans and the basis of these loans as represented by cash.

In the table which follows, I have used as a basis of calculation the figures showing loans and the extreme movements of cash into and out of New York Clearing House banks that have already been produced in the course of this article. Loans have been used instead of deposits, as the two usually correspond rather closely, and it is with loans we are primarily concerned; besides, withdrawals of cash would affect the deposits and produce a wrong showing. The results in percentages are therefore the ratios of cash to loans instead of reserves to deposits, but they can be regarded as showing, to all intents and purposes, the same thing as if deposits had been used.

I have taken the loans as I found them in each year at the maximum in August, and have assumed that no reduction be made therefrom during the following months of September, October, November and December. But, wherever expansion of loans has actually taken place in the months following August, the actual volume of loans in the month in which the expansion occurred has been taken into the calculation for that month and following months, except where there has actually been still further expansion, in which case the new maximum figures are used. By that method the years of expanding business during the months under consideration have been taken into the calculations, and, at the same time, those years in which there was enforced liquidation have been provided for.

Moral Effects of the Measure.

The table, therefore, shows what might have been done with the loans in the years examined if the national banking law permitted some flexibility in reserve requirements as applied to "central reserve" banks. In all cases, excepting 1907, we would have been able to release cash to the interior with the same freedom, while at the same time we could have maintained the maximum loans of August, or even expanded them in some instances, without passing below the 20% mark. Even in 1907, which was an exceptional year in more ways than one, we would have come through without reducing loans so drastically

TABLE SHOWING THAT IT WOULD NOT HAVE BEEN NECESSARY TO REDUCE LOA[NS] DURING THE CROP MOVING PERIOD IF THE BANKS HAD BEEN PERMITTED BY L[AW] TO OPERATE ON A REDUCED RESERVE BASIS DURING THE MONTHS OF SEPTEMB[ER], OCTOBER, NOVEMBER AND DECEMBER IN THE YEARS 1902 TO 1912 INCLUSIVE.

	Jan.	Feb.	Mar.	Apr.	May.	June.	July.	Aug.	Sept.	Oct.	Nov.
1902—Cash	$261	$266	$245	$242	$241	$251	$253	$243	$220	$238	$244
Loans	869	936	938	893	870	893	913	*929	874	865	879
% Cash								26.1	23.6	25.6	26.2
% Cash on basis of August loans:											
1903—Cash	260	244	227	224	238	228	244	249	239	240	214
Loans	904	950	904	900	928	903	917	*923	917	907	880
% Cash								26.9	25.8	26.0	23.1
% Cash on basis of August loans:											
1904—Cash	280	288	289	311	288	323	357	360	328	313	293
Loans	994	999	1,007	1,049	1,078	1,036	1,099	*1,099	*1,140	*1,145	1,102
% Cash								32.7	28.7	27.3	25.6
% Cash on basis of August, September and October loans:											
1905—Cash	324	307	294	290	304	290	315	304	276	266	252
Loans	1,115	1,142	1,109	1,090	1,120	1,089	1,144	*1,146	1,071	1,026	1,012
% Cash								26.5	24.0	23.2	21.9
% Cash on basis of August loans:											
1906—Cash	246	276	256	248	266	274	283	267	246	275	248
Loans	1,041	1,061	1,019	1,009	1,049	1,060	1,036	*1,077	1,036	*1,082	1,039
% Cash								24.8	22.9	25.4	22.9
% Cash on basis of August and October loans:											
1907—Cash	282	265	254	288	293	275	283	270	268	267	215
Loans	1,085	1,099	1,049	1,123	1,140	1,126	1,104	*1,126	1,088	1,076	*1,198
% Cash								23.9	23.8	23.7	17.9
% Cash on basis of August and November loans:											
1908—Cash	318	325	337	371	383	367	396	414	401	385	379
Loans	1,117	1,161	1,164	1,195	1,219	1,239	1,270	*1,290	*1,322	*1,338	*1,347
% Cash								32.1	30.3	28.7	28.1
% Cash on basis of August to November loans:											
1909—Cash	383	354	351	357	374	386	390	369	345	321	303
Loans	1,341	1,316	1,298	1,339	1,331	1,372	1,340	*1,361	1,316	1,233	1,196
% Cash								27.1	25.3	23.5	22.2
% Cash on basis of August loans:											

and still we would have had left a fair margin over the 15% suggested for the month of November. And, looking at the psychological aspect of the matter, the moral effect of such an amendment to the national banking law as has been suggested would have been of incalculable value during those troublous days, particularly if it had been in existence for a few years and its practicability fully demonstrated. If such a law had been on the statutes, no one would have felt alarmed when they saw reserves falling below 25% of deposits, and they would not have accentuated the acuteness of the situation by withdrawing cash and hiding it away in safe deposit boxes and under carpets and mattresses, as was the case in the latter part of 1907.

In the year 1907 the maximum cash holdings of New York Clearing House banks reached $288,000,000 in round numbers in May. In July they were $283,000,000. In August, they had dwindled to $270,000,000 and held rather close to that figure during September and October. The big drop came in November, when the minimum $215,000,000 was reached. This latter figure by no means represents the full drain upon New York Clearing House banks at that time. If we deduct the importations of gold during November, which amounted to $62,000,000, the decrease in cash from the July figures amounts to $130,000,000. As the figures stand, the decrease was $68,000,000. In December, an additional $43,000,000 gold was imported. New York bankers began early in the year to prepare for an enormous fall and winter business. The whole of the preceding year was one of full employment of money in general business and in speculation. The 25% reserves were maintained with great difficulty during the last four months of 1906, and the fluctuations in the loans were violent. In the early part of 1907, although cash holdings rose rapidly, there was a slump in them during February and March, and, in order to strengthen their position, liquidation was enforced during March which reduced loans $50,000,000. After that, cash holdings again rose to above the former levels of the year, and fluctuated within comparatively narrow limits until the pinch came in November.

The panic of 1907, which reached its height (or depth) in November, was essentially a banking panic and was due wholly to *loss of confidence* on the part of the frightened depositors. It would have been mitigated or might possibly have been avoided altogether if the "central reserve" banks could have had the *moral backing* of a law permitting a more free use of their reserves in meeting the withdrawals of depositors. The average depositor gives very little consideration to the volume or percentage of reserves his bank may be carrying, so long as he is able to draw his cash without difficulty. Innumerable instances could be cited where, during the course of a run on a bank, depositors have drawn their money at one window and immediately redeposited it at another. In Chicago a good many years ago, when a run started on the banks, the sight of the money handed out to a depositor upon presentation of his pass book, impressed him so deeply that he asked the paying teller to take the money back. He was told that he must take the money and see the receiving teller about redepositing it. The institution, a savings bank, not only saved a lot of interest by that action, but also started thereby a wave of confidence which resulted in an abrupt ending of the threatened disastrous run on that bank and other banks in the city.

The trouble in 1907 was accentuated by the bad practices and subsequent failure of several banking institutions, but even these failures and the effects thereof could have been minimized if the amendment suggested had been in force. The bank official no less than the depositor becomes timid when he faces the alternative of running counter to the letter of the law or taking a tighter grip on the hard cash in order to maintain the lawful reserve. And, if he cannot manage to retain the cash, he calls in loans, which is one more means of inspiring fear in the minds of the public. A large part of the loss of confidence in that year was due to the slashes in the loans which were made necessary by the rigid reserve requirements. If these reserve requirments had been more flexible and, consequently, little or no disturbance of the loans had been necessary, apprehension over the situation would have been lessened proportionately, and the chances are the banks would not have been compelled to refuse payment in currency or to resort to the use of Clearing House certificates.

It is my firm belief that we give too little consideration to the importance of maintaining bank loans on a fairly stable level, taking into consideration the gradual upward climb in the volume of the business of the country. In conversation with one of the active heads of a great New York bank, a few days ago, I was told (what everybody knows) that big banks do not hesitate to go below 25% when necessary, and he added that his bank at that moment was down to 22½%. He admitted, however, that they would not dare take advantage of the 30 days' limit or remain in that condition for even one week. But his concluding remark was quite significant, "We drop below 25%—for a day or two when necessary rather than frighten people by calling a lot of loans in one day."

When the average man sees the banks calling loans and interest rates going up, his first and most natural thought is that they are losing cash, and that would usually be correct. If it is carried very far or too precipitately, he begins to wonder if his little account is safe, and it needs but little more to cause the uneasiness to develop into positive panic which leads him to the paying teller's window. Multiply this individual state of mind by thousands or tens of thousands and you have the making of another 1907 experience.

If this proposed amendment providing for a sliding scale of reserve requirements, during the definitely known annual crop-moving period of strain, will eliminate the anxiety over loans, and, consequently, lessen the danger of loss of confidence, a great deal will have been accomplished by its enactment.

Possible Objections to the Measure.

It may be argued that it would be dangerous to reduce present reserve requirements at any time, and that our "central reserve" banks ought to carry as large a percentage of reserves as the Bank of England or the Bank of France, 40 or 50% or even as high as 60%. The answer to that objection is that, in the cases cited, the *responsibility is centralized* in one bank, whereas in this country, the responsibility is *divided* among 55 institutions. These 55 banks have a capitalization of about $185,-000,000; surplus of about $163,000,000, and, according to the current Comptroller's report, undivided profits of about $48,000,000. The fact that the responsibility is thus divided is in one sense an element of strength, for, while the absence of unanimity of action is sometimes to be deplored, the policy of these banks is not subject to the judgment of one man or set of men, and their affiliations are sufficiently close to be a guarantee that danger in any single quarter will be met with practically united action from other quarters. Furthermore, the functions of the Bank of England and the Bank of France are of a more international character than is the case with the American banks. They are also Government banks and hold the Treasury gold stock.

It may also be argued that the plan is not sufficiently broad; that it does not provide for unexpected calls upon the resources of the banks that may be made outside of the crop-moving period. That is true, but the objection does not alter the value of its application to the period when we know we are most likely to encounter rough weather. We now have some of the bad spots charted and it will not do to disregard them because of uncharted rocks that may exist in the financial seas. In the tables and charts already submitted, it will be noted that the month of March is usually a month of strain, and it might be well to extend the application of the plan to that month also. A little further along in this article, another proposition will be advanced which will assist in taking care of any sudden or unexpected strain, or demand for currency outside of the regularly recurring seasonal demands.

The objection to the general application of

this plan to all months of the year, in my opinion, is the absence of regularity and the consequent bad effect upon confidence. The records do not show the presence of any regularly recurring period of strain outside the crop-moving time, excepting the month of March. The strain in March does not last long and loans are not seriously disturbed thereby. The value of this plan, as I see it, lies in its application to a regularly recurring period when its purpose would be fully understood by everybody, and when its application would be accepted with *perfect confidence.*

Still another objection to the plan that might be made, is the fear that during the period when the plan is in operation, it may turn out that the call for money from the outside banks is considerably less insistent than usual, and, as a consequence speculators would be tempted to utilize the increased loaning facilities created by the operation of the plan. This objection could be met by inserting a clause in the law prohibiting the "central reserve" banks and "reserve banks" from expanding their loans beyond a certain percentage during the period when the plan was in operation. That would prevent the banks from fostering unwise and reckless speculation and from taking advantage of the law for purposes other than which it was intended. This clause, however, should be so worded that, if the "central reserve" and "reserve banks" should see fit to import gold for the purpose of increasing their credit facilities, the prohibition with regard to expansion of loans would be modified in accordance with the extent of the importations. In other words, so long as the banks could show reserves in excess of 25%, the prohibition would not be considered as in force. But as soon as their reserves fall below 25% in taking advantage of the law, the loan expansion must stop or at least be restricted within certain limits. That would also provide for shipments of currency from the country during the prescribed period.

A further objection that might be offered hinges on the proposition that usually the country banks draw upon the reserve centers for the purpose of increasing their credit facilities as much if not more than they do for the purpose of obtaining an additional supply of circulating medium; that if additional circulation was all that was needed, they could utilize their privilege of increasing their national bank note circulation, or, for that matter, while the Aldrich-Vreeland law is in force, they could make use of the emergency currency. In answer to this, I would respectfully call attention to the fact that the country banks have been exercising their privilege in the matter of United States bond secured circulation, otherwise known as national bank notes, for a good many years, and that the volume of this sort of circulating medium has steadily expanded from about $200,000,000 in 1896 to over $700,000,000 at the present time; yet, we are subjected with ever-recurring regularity to the same old money strain, in varying degrees of intensity according as business is good or bad or crops heavy or light, year after year. The trouble with this sort of currency is that, once it is issued, it seldom comes in for redemption until it is worn out, and in the end, after making due allowance for the natural growth of the country, it spells inflation. If this sort of currency could be recalled promptly when the necessity for it had passed, the evil effects of inflation would be obviated, but that is a measure that has not yet been devised to the entire satisfaction of all the interests concerned. Besides, the limit of circulation based on the Government bonds now in existence has been about reached, and emergency currency is not available except at prohibitive rates. So far as the need of additional credit facilities is concerned, when the country banks call for shipments of currency, they are almost invariably supplied with the real article—money that is eligible for their reserves if it is needed for that purpose.

While we are on this subject of national bank notes, let us see what a little examination will bring to light.

National Bank Notes.

It probably never will be definitely known to whom the credit for the first conception of a government bond secured currency is due. Neither is it entirely clear from the records what was the ruling motive or purpose of those who were responsible for its creation through act of Congress. Salmon P. Chase, who was Secretary of the Treasury in those troublous times, is generally credited with being the father of the measure which brought into being the present national banking system and its accompanying bank note currency system. It is certain that without his great activity in the matter, our present comparatively satisfactory banking system would never have seen the light of day. It would either have died in the borning or its birth delayed for many years. In a space of time, which, though it must have seemed inordinately long at that time, was incredibly short when we consider the flight of time since then and the opposition to the measure, he accomplished what might easily have taken decades of slow evolution to bring forth.

The idea itself was not altogether new. It was, to some extent, an adaptation of the system then in vogue in some of the States, notably New York State, whereby banks operating under State charters were given bank note issuing privileges based upon security in the shape of State bonds deposited with the State Treasurer. The novelty of the idea was in its nation-wide application. For State bonds, Secretary Chase proposed the substitution of United States Government bonds, and the replacement of State supervision by national supervision. The measure was thus subjected to more or less hostility from State authorities because of the possible derangement of the market for State bond issues. The State banks themselves bitterly opposed the measure on these and other grounds.

But, the necessity for the measure was very great, and Secretary Chase eventually succeeded in enlisting the invincible Sherman in the cause, and the thing was accomplished. The necessity which furnished the motive for Secretary Chase's efforts was two-fold—that of providing a market for government bonds for the purpose of securing money with which to carry on the war against the secessionists, and the correction of the intolerable evils connected with the then existing currency which was circulating in the guise of money. Which of the two considerations were the more important at that time is difficult to determine off-hand. It seems, however, that successful flotation of Government bonds depended no less upon the standardization of the currency than the standardization of the currency depended upon its divorce from State supervision. It was almost impossible to raise anything but depreciated money for use by the Government except by going abroad for it. The reason for this was that the State laws were so lax and so uncertain, and so lacking in uniformity that it was possible in a great many States for absolutely irresponsible persons to obtain charters and issue currency at their own sweet will and put it into circulation in other localities—money which even lacked the saving grace of good printing and engraving, to say nothing of value. Consequently, the people, who would have aided the Government with their money, had nothing but worthless money to offer, as the redundancy of worthless or depreciated currency had forced specie out of the country to a point of practical depletion. And, under the then prevailing conditions, the banks could not afford to extend aid except at rates which were ruinous to the Government. The act creating the present national banking system and a standardized national bank note Government bond secured currency was passed on June 3, 1864, and there it has stood ever since, with some modifications, up to the present time. It was admirably conceived to meet the exigencies of the day, but, in so far as the privilege of issuing bank notes produces inflation of the currency, we are still paying the penalty of the civil war. But, as an offset, we got rid of the war, and one of the most abominable currency systems ever experienced by any mod-

ern country, and established banking upon a
sound basis.

Bank Note Redemption Fund.

A recital of the various changes in the law
regarding the volume of bank notes which may
be issued, the geographical distribution of the
same, the terms on which they may be issued
and the reserve fund to be kept on hand for
their redemption, would consume more space
than is available. As the law now reads, the
banks are required to keep on deposit with the
Treasurer of the United States a fund equal to
5% of their national bank note issue, the
amount so deposited to be counted in their reserves. According to the current report of the
Comptroller of the Currency this fund amounted to over $35,000,000, of which $23,000,000
comes from the country banks, $8,000,000 from
the "reserve" banks and about $4,000,000 from
the "central reserve" banks. Thus, it will be
seen that whatever advantage accrues from the
privilege of counting this redemption fund in
the reserves is more largely enjoyed by the
country banks than all the rest of the banks
together. Inasmuch as the bulk of the redemption of these notes is between banks, there is
no great necessity for a redemption fund, and,
furthermore, the notes are backed by deposits
of Government bonds which ought to be sufficient. However, I will not argue that point.
The important point to be considered is that
this fund is in the hands of the Treasurer of
the United States and is doing only a portion
of the work that it might accomplish. Reserves
against deposits, to a certain extent, may be
passed along from one class of banks to the
next highest, thereby being made available for

additional work. If this redemption fund was treated in the same manner as reserves against deposits, 60% of the $23,000,000 belonging to the country banks could be passed along to the "reserve" banks, and 50% of that $13,800,000, together with 50% of the $8,000,000 belonging to the "reserve" banks, a total of over $10,000,-000, could be utilized by the "central reserve" banks. As the matter now stands, we are employing $31,000,000 of this money in the redemption fund in a most un-economical manner. Perhaps the easiest and most satisfactory method of dealing with this fund would be to leave it in the hands of the Treasurer of the United States and endow him with the power to mobilize the fund for use in any quarter where a stringency is threatened at any time. This vast sum judicially used at the right time and in the right place, and withdrawn at the proper time would provide us with a means of maintaining an equilibrium that would be of great service during out-of-season periods of strain. It will be remembered that $25,000,000 poured into the money market in 1907 was the means of turning the tide, and stopped the panic which threatened to pass beyond all human control The Government, of course, did a great deal more than that in the way of deposits with the banks, but the efficiency of these deposits was lessened by the hesitating manner in which they were made. The stringency was allowed to become too acute before the corrective was administered. If the Secretary of the Treasury or some other public official or committee of officials had had the authority and a definite sum of money to work with in 1907, much of the loss of confidence would have been avoided. The Government is in more or less active partnership with the banks, for it has reaped a great many benefits from the present system of banking and currency, and it ought to put a representative, or a committee representing it, in a position to perform prompt and active service at all times. It should extend aid at the inception of trouble, not at its crisis. If there is stringency in Hoboken, there is the place to apply the remedy; it takes too long for the medicine to reach Hoboken if it is applied in Kalamazoo or Podunk.

With a sliding scale of reserves in the "reserve" and "central reserve" cities and a mobilized fund in the hands of a competent Government official, much of the inconvenience and the danger attendant upon a rigid, inelastic currency would be avoided, and the chances of a recurrence of another 1907 would be greatly lessened.

CHAPTER VII.

Our Foreign Trade.

The condition of our foreign trade and the balance created abroad by our shipments of merchandise, specie and securities is an important factor bearing on security prices. It is ordinarily the case that our exports of merchandise receive attention to the exclusion of the other items mentioned, but it is important that all should be considered.

One point which is often misunderstood and which causes undue apprehension in examining the record of exports is the gradual falling off in our sales of foodstuffs. Our foreign sales of grain have fallen off rapidly and will probably continue to do so, but that is nothing to be alarmed about.

It is the history of all new countries that in their infancy they have sold what they produced from the soil and purchased manufactured goods. Gradually this changes until in time the process is reversed. In many cases lawmakers have foolishly attempted to change these conditions by legislation. England had a stormy career in this direction and flopped around helplessly for years before a clear understanding was obtained. In the decade from 1851 to 1860, 51.2 per cent. of our total imports was in manufactures and only 21.3 per cent in raw materials for use in manufactures. In 1901 24.9% of our total imports was manufactured goods and 45.6% raw materials and partly manufactured goods. During the same period our imports of foodstuffs declined somewhat and our exports of foodstuffs increased. This was due to the great increase in farming during the half century, but that increase has come nearer to reaching its limitations now and we may expect to see our exports of manufactures rise indefinitely with some fluctuations from time to time. The percentages following show the changes in imports and exports during the last decade:

Table Showing Imports of Merchandise 1901 to 1910 Inclusive in Percentages.

	Manufactures	Raw Materials & Unfinished Manufactures	Foodstuffs
1901	24.9%	45.6%	28.7%
1902	25.6%	49.9%	23.8%
1903	25.1%	51.2%	23.0%
1904	25.5%	48.5%	25.2%
1905	22.6%	50.7%	26.0%
1906	25.1%	51.7%	22.4%
1907	25.4%	52.3%	21.5%
1908	27.8%	46.8%	24.5%
1909	22.8%	51.3%	25.1%
1910	23.9%	55.3%	20.0%

Table Showing Exports of Merchandise 1901 to 1910 Inclusive in Percentages.

	Manufactures	Raw Materials & Unfinished Manufactures	Foodstuffs
1901	31.8%	27.2%	39.9%
1902	33.4%	27.5%	37.9%
1903	33.6%	29.3%	36.5%
1904	36.4%	32.2%	31.0%
1905	41.0%	31.7%	26.9%
1906	39.9%	29.1%	30.5%
1907	39.9%	32.0%	27.7%
1908	40.9%	30.3%	28.4%
1909	41.0%	31.8%	26.7%
1910	43.0%	34.4%	22.0%

We are rapidly approaching the point when we will no longer be exporters of foodstuffs on balance, but our manufactures will make up for that.

Cotton is the principal item in our exports of other than manufactured goods. It is called our "money" crop and so great is the revenue from the staple that it now makes up almost 30% (in dollars) of our total merchandise balance. The money received for our exports of cotton has increased rapidly in late years, partly because of an increase in production and exports, and partly because of a gradual upward trend in prices in common with all other commodities. In 1871 we exported less than 2,000,000 bales of cotton; in 1881 over 3,000,000 bales; in 1891 almost 6,000,000 bales; in 1901 almost 7,000,000 bales, and in 1908 over 9,000,000 bales. In twenty years the average price received for exported cotton has risen from about 8 cents per pound to about 11 cents per pound. It is probable that increase in production will continue for some time to come, but in a slower ratio. Scientific farming will be added and further increase in acreage and larger crops will follow. As the world is largely dependent on us for her cotton, and as population is increasing more rapidly than production, it is not reasonable to expect any material decline in the price level except in the way of fluctuations. The trend of all commodity prices is also upward and will so continue as long as gold production continues to increase. One of the most surprising things about cotton and one of the greatest sources of economic waste is the practice of shipping raw cotton abroad and importing the goods manufactured therefrom. This error will be cured in time. There are already evidences of an understanding of the situation and an attempt to rectify it.

Our exports of specie do not enter very largely into our trade balances as compared with merchandise exports. Since 1873 we have sold abroad on balance about 9 billion dollars of merchandise and $500,000,000 of specie.

Our sales of securities abroad present a different aspect from that of merchandise and specie. Merchandise goes into consumption, and the same may be said in a modified way of specie. The securities, however, must be repaid at maturity and in addition to this we pay interest and dividends on such rented capital between the dates of issue and maturity. There are no dependable statistics as to the amounts of our securities held abroad, but some of the estimates should come pretty close to the truth. "The London Statist" recently estimated England's holdings of our securities at about three billion dollars and interest thereon at the rate of 4.5%, or about $130,000,000 per annum. The editor's estimate of the total foreign capital in this country is about six billion dollars.

It is frequently the case that this large indebtedness to foreigners and the consequent drain in the form of interest and dividends is viewed with alarm, and the apprehension is fostered by pessimists or radicals who have only a hazy idea of what such indebtedness represents. The money so borrowed merely represents capital employed in the development of our industries and resources. It is reasonable to assume that when a railroad or other great corporation places $50,000,000 of bonds abroad, it is because they expect to employ that sum to advantage, to reap enough from its use to pay the interest and make a profit for themselves before the loan matures. In this regard it may be noted that we hear much talk about the large sums we expend annually for freights in foreign bottoms. To hear these agitators harp on the fact that we have no merchant marine and no laws to encourage such enterprises, one would think the freights paid to foreign vessel owners was a dead loss. An examination of the earnings of ocean transportation companies will show that the return on such investments is not large, and that under present conditions our money can be more profitably employed in other directions. When the time comes that ocean freights show a great enough return as compared with other enterprises, we will soon have both the ships and the laws.

We may classify the different items which operate against our trade balance under four important heads: Interest and dividends, freights in foreign bottoms, remittances of aliens and expenditures of tourists. Estimates vary considerably, but the latest estimate at hand, that compiled by Frank Fayant, is as follows:

Interest and dividends, about.......$200,000,000
Remittances of aliens, about........ 150,000,000
Freights in foreign bottoms........ 57,000,000
Tourist expenditures 140,000,000

The following tables show our imports, exports, and trade balances of merchandise and specie for a period of years.

Merchandise Exports, Imports and Balances 1901 to 1910 Inclusive.

Years.	Exports.	Imports.	Balance.	
1901	$1,487,764,991	$823,172,165	Exp.	$664,592,826
1902	1,381,719,401	903,320,948	Exp.	478,398,453
1903	1,420,141,679	1,025,719,237	Exp.	394,422,442
1904	1,460,827,271	991,087,371	Exp.	469,739,900
1905	1,518,561,666	1,117,513,071	Exp.	401,048,595
1906	1,743,864,500	1,226,562,446	Exp.	517,302,054
1907	1,880,851,078	1,434,421,425	Exp.	446,429,653
1908	1,860,773,346	1,194,341,792	Exp.	666,431,554
1909	1,663,011,104	1,311,920,224	Exp.	351,090,880
1910	1,744,984,720	1,557,819,988	Exp.	187,164,732

Gold Exports, Imports and Balances 1901 to 1910 Inclusive.

	Exports. Gold coin and bullion.	Imports. Gold coin and bullion.	Balance. Gold coin & bullion excess.	
1901...	$53,185,177	$66,051,187	Imp.	$12,866,010
1902...	48,568,950	52,021,254	Imp.	3,452,304
1903...	47,090,595	44,982,027	Exp.	2,108,568
1904...	81,459,986	99,055,368	Imp.	17,595,382
1905...	92,594,024	53,648,961	Exp.	38,945,063
1906...	38,573,591	96,221,730	Imp.	57,648,139
1907...	51,399,176	114,510,249	Imp.	63,111,073
1908...	72,432,924	148,337,321	Imp.	75,904,397
1909...	91,531,818	44,033,989	Exp.	47,527,829
1910...	118,563,215	43,339,905	Exp.	75,223,310

There is no intention to attempt in this chapter a long discussion of the numerous influences bearing on our foreign trade, but the foregoing paragraphs are presented so that the reader may not be deceived from time to time by the numerous scareheads about our dwindling wheat exports, our payment of ocean freights, our annual rentals for capital, etc. What is particularly considered is the more immediate effects on prices from year to year, or even from month to month, rather than the economic changes of decades or generations.

By examining the monthly documents issued by the Bureau of Statistics of the Department of Commerce and Labor, we may frequently get some interesting side lights on our financial position and the tendency to extravagance or economy. It is found that after a long period of unusual prosperity or adversity a nation does not differ much from the ordinary individual. If we see an individual who has rapidly built up a profitable business spending money freely, buying wines and diamonds or whatever, we are not slow to predict disaster, and our predictions are usually verified. If, after such excesses and mistakes, we see the same individual economizing and mending his ways, we are ready to predict a better future, and again we are usually right. The same thing is true of a nation. I may say, in passing, that I have often found this habit of contracting a large question to individual proportions, or of considering one share of the stock of a great corporation by itself instead of as a member of a large family, to be very helpful. We often become confused and amazed by an exhibit of figures which stagger us, while the proposition appears simple enough if resolved into smaller proportions. This process of diminution is purely a mental phase, but the contracted fact fits the head better.

So let us look at the personal habits of Uncle Sam during one of his prosperous periods, and one of his periods of rehabilitation. A simple example, and the most recent, is that of the period between 1905 and 1908. In 1906 and 1907 our exports of merchandise were larger than at any time in history, but imports expanded so rapidly that our trade balance did not keep step with the increase in exports. In July and August of 1907 our exports only exceeded imports by a slight margin. Looking at the *character* of the imports, extravagance, incited by prosperity, is immediately apparent. Let us take two luxuries for example, precious stones and champagne.

Imports of Precious Stones and Champagne for a Period of Years.

	Precious stones.	Champagne.
1904	$23,626,608	$4,969,635
1905	33,761,506	5,723,764
1906	40,380,762	6,127,062
1907	42,468,022	6,228,280
1908	16,714,137	5,221,070

It was so in almost all lines representing luxuries. Even in perfumed soaps we saved over a
quarter of a million in 1908 as compared with
1907. Although our exports in 1908 were not so
large as in 1907 by $170,000,000, our trade bal-
ances broke all records, being $136,000,000 in ex-
cess of 1907.

If these exhibits are examined by months instead of by years, the figures are even more strik-
ing, for it was in the latter part of 1906 and the
early part of 1907 that extravagance reached its
height, and improvement began to show long before the end of 1907. The nation acted just like
our hypothetical individual, with the same results.

Exports and imports of gold are not so important as those of merchandise, and the movements
are as a general rule seasonal. We may naturally
expect to ship some gold in the first half of the
year, and import in the latter half. Danger is indicated when we are parting with our gold or
borrowing gold abroad in a period of high prices
and extravagance. In the panics which have followed such conditions we have always managed
to get gold to relieve us, but we have always had
to pay a high price for it. In 1906 we imported
$108,000,000 more gold than we exported, and
in 1907, at the time when such imports should
naturally have ceased and a return flow set in,
we were in such a pickle that it was imperative
that we import largely again. In that year we
received $88,182,000 gold more than we exported,
but we gained this gold by great sacrifices in our
prices of merchandise and securities. We sold
things for less than they were worth because we
had to have the money. In 1908 and 1909 we exported about $120,000,000 more gold than we im-
ported, as the need for it had ended. The same

thing happened in a modified manner preceding
and following the panic of 1903, and has been in
evidence in all former panic periods. In regard
to gold exports, we can again bring in the
hypothetical individual who bought diamonds
and wine. When he is receiving gold for what
he has to sell in excess of his expenditures, he
is all right, but if thsi money is only temporarily in his hands, and instead of being able to
repay it the next year, he is forced to borrow
more, he will do so at a sacrifice. When he
does manage to settle up, he will do better.
That is what occurred to the nation in 1906 to
1909.

CHAPTER VIII.

Bank Clearings.

In determining the progress of general business our bank clearings furnish the most satisfactory barometer. In ordinary times increases and decreases in clearings are seasonal, closely following the interest rates on money. The natural period of advancing volume of clearings is the latter half of the year, and they usually fall off during the first half of the year. Comparisons with a preceding year or years will show correctly therefore, while comparisons of one month with the preceding month are often misleading. A comparison of October or November, 1907, with the same months in 1906 and other preceding years, would show a great falling off in business activity, and that instead of advancing in volume in these months, clearings had fallen off. This represented stagnation in business in the last stages of the 1907 panic. It was noticeable, however, that the improvement in business as represented by volume of clearings in 1908 began much earlier than might ordinarily be expected. This recuperation began in February, 1908, and continued to the end of the year without a seasonal midyear reaction of any importance. The same thing was true in 1909, and by January, 1910, volume of clearings had reached the highest point in history. All through the years 1908 and 1909 it was plain that the lost ground of 1907 was being rapidly recovered and this was faithfully reflected in the course of security prices.

Clearings outside of New York frequently

fall, while New York clearings are rising, and vice versa; but this is usually due to natural causes, such as the activity during the crop seasons, etc. The best plan is to consult total clearings which are published weekly and monthly. By so doing we may determine whether or not the stories of business depression or activity are true. It is invariably the case, after a period of depression, that many people cannot and will not admit that business is fair and is improving steadily and healthily. They do not recognize the truth until the recovery is at its height and is so plain that it cannot be refuted. These people draw mental comparisons of the orderly betterment of the present with the undue inflation of the past, or allow their views to be circumscribed by personal experience. An intelligent examination of the volume of clearings from time to time will show with remarkable accuracy the state and progress of business.

In the panic of 1893 the volume of clearings fell off badly, as was to be expected. There was some desultory recovery in 1894 and 1895, but it was below normal and entirely unsatisfactory. The recovery of security prices was also slow. In 1896 clearings fell almost as low as in 1893, a very bad state of affairs as the volume of money employed should, of course, grow gradually greater from year to year. Security prices reflected these conditions and reached a lower level than in 1893. It was entirely different after the panics of 1903 and 1907. In both cases rapid recuperation in general business was shown by steadily increasing clearings and the stock market advanced in both cases.

The course of security prices and bank clearings follow or accompany each other so faithfully that they may, in charted form, be superimposed without any radical variations one from the other. The security prices show a moderate precession. It would be folly, therefore, to buy stocks merely because clearings are very large, as they may have reached the pinnacle, in which case security prices would have reached their apex ahead of business conditions. What can be determined is the present state of general business and the stability and character of the growth. Improvement is sometimes entirely too rapid for safety—a mushroom growth. Sometimes a seasonal recovery is only perfunctory and does not come up to what might reasonably be expected. On the other hand a seasonable decline will not be so great as it would be under ordinary circumstances, which would show an improving trend sufficient to absorb a portion of the natural reaction. That was the case in 1908 and 1909.

It is sometimes the case that bank clearings make a somewhat false showing because of activity or dulness on the stock exchanges. General business may be slowly improving, but a period of stagnation in stock exchange transactions will reduce the total amount of clearings. On the other hand general business may have halted or be receding slowly, and large speculative transactions on the exchanges will artificially swell the volume of clearings. This fact can be easily discovered and estimated by consulting the record of sales on the New York Stock Exchange and other prominent bourses.

The total bank clearings by months for a series of years are given herewith:

Bank Clearings by Months—1901-1911.

(Last six figures omitted.)

	Jan.	Feb.	Mch.	April	May	June	July	August	Sept.	Oct.	Nov.
1901..	$10,720	$8,363	$10,007	$12,015	$12,831	$10,109	$9,369	$ 7,790	$7,971	$9,536	$9,853
1902..	1 0665	8,363	8,892	1 099	10,392	8,217	10,179	8,952	10,166	11,366	10,096
1903..	11,088	8,468	9,582	9,581	9,118	9,422	9,709	7,921	7,673	9,176	8,169
1904..	9,436	7,713	8,383	8,809	8,215	8,058	8,660	8,008	8,844	11,509	12,505
1905..	11,848	10,650	12,918	12,735	12,059	10,815	10,866	10,902	10,885	12,624	1 149
1906..	16,321	12,462	12,993	12,884	13,218	12,230	11,639	13,131	12,497	11,529	13,633
1907..	15,054	11,823	14,657	12,661	12,406	1 159	12,372	11,558	10,573	13,804	9,679
1908..	11,359	8,756	9,777	9,764	10,858	9,825	11,071	10,248	11,112	12,136	12,976
1909..	14,052	11,260	12,623	13,962	1 306	14,155	13,469	13,510	13,542	15,871	14,786
1910..	17,143	13,111	15,021	11,014	13,147	13,811	13,285	11,508	11,361	13,787	13,595
1911..	14,444	12,249	13,449	12,380	13,503	13,812	13,052	12,646	12,589	13,545	......

CHAPTER IX.

Charts and Stop Loss Orders.

The losses made annually through the following of charts and the employment of stop loss orders make up a very large total. In speaking of charts I refer to the numerous devices employed as a basis of mechanical speculation and not in any way to economic charts of conditions, etc. These latter are merely convenient methods of picturing history and are of great service to the student or investigator. If we decide, for example, that a high ratio of loans to deposits, together with a low ratio of specie to loans is a dangerous state of affairs, we may more easily confirm the effect of such conditions in the past and ascertain how serious the effects have been, by reference to properly prepared charts than by laboriously digging out records from numerous volumes. In order to have all salient statistics bearing on price movements at hand we must have a library of many hundreds of volumes covering a long period of years, in which the data we require is concealed in a mass of other matter. Also we find it necessary, in the interest of accuracy, to check and confirm every exhibit so compiled, as tabulated exhibits often contain errors, and statistical work based on errors is worse than useless. By the use of a scientific and carefully prepared set of charts we avoid all this labor. The work is done for us by competent men and the salient statistics are visualized in the scope of a few hundred pages.

But the class of charts which is criticised herein is an attempt, taking several different forms, to invent and successfully employ a "system" such as we find on race tracks or in gambling houses. We have yet to find a single instance of a considerable sum being accumulated by such methods. At times the exponents of chart systems have a more or less extended period of success, but this is usually accidental and is followed by reversals.

One of the simplest and most common chart methods consists of drawing a picture of the market for a long period of years and operating on the theory that history will repeat itself indefinitely. It is a matter of common logic to say that the longer a merely fortuitous parallel is continued the nearer we are to divergence. The course of the stock market from 1896 to 1902 was continually upward with only moderate reversals which usually occurred in the latter part of the year. This gave rise to our greatest crop of chart players. The demonstration on paper looked peculiarly convincing and found many followers, particularly when the promoters were shrewd enough not to go back further than 1896. But alas, just as sufficient precedent had been found for a basic formula, the panic of 1903 appeared and all the golden dreams were dissipated. The flaw lay in the fact that the charts did not take cognizance of changed conditions. Such changes would have been recognized if the time spent in preparing charts had been devoted to a careful examination of fundamentals instead of devising a mechanical system.

Following the downfall of the repetition theory as set forth above, many attempts at improvement in methods were made. The number of shares were counted from day to day and it was argued that if a certain stock advanced steadily on total purchases of, say one million shares, and then hesitated or began declining, it was reasonable to assume that the former purchases were now being disposed of and that a decline would follow. This theory worked, as all such theories do, often enough to inspire the confidence of the believers, and it failed often enough to prevent profits or create losses. The hesitation might be merely a natural plateau of prices, or might be due to some moderate profit taking, or to a desire to discourage undesirable followers, or whatever; in which case the buying and the advancing trend was soon resumed.

Chart players attach much importance to "double tops" and "double bottoms." The theory in this case is that if a certain stock or the general market advances rapidly to say an average price of $100 per share, then declines to say $95, resumes the advance and again reaches $100, it is time to watch for a definite indication of the trend of the market. If the market again stops at the double top and begins declining, a considerable break may be expected. If, however, the market continues to advance and goes through the double top to say an average of $102 or $103, it is assumed that the trend will continue upward, and that purchases are warranted at the high level.

There is some elementary basis for this form of reasoning but it is entirely insufficient. When the market originally advanced to 100 there were a good many speculative buyers around the top, and the decline of five points which followed discouraged them. The first thing a discouraged speculator makes up his mind to is that he will get out even as soon as he can and when the double top is made, there is frequently enough of this selling to cause hesitation or give a declining impetus. If such selling is absorbed at once and the advance continues, it is reasoned that there is a good demand for the specific security, or for securities generally. To say nothing of the illogical end of the matter, which consists of waiting for higher prices before buying, there are two flaws in the theory. Both are due to its increasing popularity and use by the chart followers. If one man or a few men had evolved and followed the plan, some profits might be reaped, but when a horde of indiscriminate operators follow it, it defeats its own ends. Not only will an influx of such buying create a bad technical condition which will weaken the market and attract bearish raids, but it will lead important operators to help drive away a large and dangerous public following. It may also be pointed out that shrewd manipulators are fully aware of the growth of this popular method and they sometimes boost prices through the "double top" by main strength merely to influence the buying which will follow.

Finding that the mechanical action of the market could not be depended on, the manufacturers and inventors of charts have elaborated their plans by using the stop loss order as an auxiliary or protective measure. The stop loss order is, in my opinion, an abomination in most cases, and a superlative abomination when used in connection with charts. It is a form of insurance which does not insure anything and is frequently productive of loss. The so-called stop loss order is employed in connection with charts in three ways: To protect paper profits already acquired; to limit actual losses on the original purchase or sale; and as a basis for original commitments.

In the protection of paper profits the method is employed as follows: A purchase is made at say 100. The market advances to 105. The purchaser places an order to sell his stock at say 103, which is called a "2 point stop." If the market declines to 103 and his stock is sold, he has retained a profit of 3 points. If the market continues to advance without reaching his selling price of 103 he "raises the stop." That is, if the price goes to 110 he will place his stop at 108 and so on. The term "stop loss" is obviously a misnomer in this case, but that is the common phraseology.

In using the stop loss order to limit losses the purchaser places his selling order at the same time he buys his stock. He buys at say 100 and gives an order to sell if the market declines to 98, on the theory that if the decline is continued he will lose only two points. The same thing of course applies to short sales. In case of a sale, the selling order at 100 would be accompanied by a stop loss order at 102.

As a basis of an original commitment the stop loss order is placed when there is no outstanding trade, either long or short. In this case the term is again a misnomer. Many people are not acquainted with the fact that such orders can be given, but they are widely used and are understood by all brokers.

The chart player or theorist who believes that if a market goes upward into new ground it will continue to advance will give an initial order to buy if higher prices are reached. Suppose the former high price has been 100 and the "double top" has been made. The idea being that if the price goes to 102 the trend will continue upward, the speculator places a "stop loss" order to buy at 102 in case that price is reached.

About the only good word that can be said for stop loss orders is in the case where they are used for protecting profits, and even for such purposes it is only occasionally that their use is warranted. There are sometimes market movements which carry prices up to, and beyond the level which should reasonably be established—that is to say, prices are higher than values. In a time of speculative excitement prices may continue to go upward and the speculator may wish to continue his commitments in order to take advantage of this fictitious advance. The stop loss order may prove helpful at such times, but it is questionable if anyone is justified in continuing purchases at all on any basis except that prices may be expected to advance because present or potential values are greater than existing prices. Under such circumstances a decline is inevitable, and may occur in such a manner as to render the stop loss order useless, as will be explained hereafter.

Stop loss orders placed with the original commitment, or as a purchasing order above the market, are intensely illogical. The only genuine and sufficient reason for buying a stock is because it is low in price and may be expected to advance. This being the case, how absurd it appears that a purchaser should buy something, presumably because it is cheap, and immediately give an order to sell in case it be-

comes cheaper. Fluctuations of a few points
are matters of weekly occurrence and have no
bearing on the trend of the market or the ultimate price reached. The stop loss order used
as above is the exact reverse of the scale order,
which contemplates a purchase at a certain
level and increasing the purchase on moderate
declines. The scale order purchaser, instead of
placing an order to sell on a two point decline,
places an order to increase his original purchase
if such a reaction appears. By so doing the
scale order operator takes advantage of natural
recessions while the stop loss operator suffers
from them. If the original purchase is based on
the only legitimate reason for buying; i. e., that
the security is cheap and may be expected to
advance in value and price, every little decline
is a distinct advantage. It may be added that
the scale order is the only mechanical method
which appears to have any merit whatever, and
is the only one employed by important operators.

The use of the stop loss order as a basis for
original purchases conflicts with all business or
speculative common sense. It contemplates
waiting to purchase a security until after the
price has advanced. (Of course the illustrations given refer to short sales as well as purchases.) If a stock is cheap at 100 why should
we wait until it goes to 102 or 103 before purchasing?

The whole theory of stop loss orders is fallacious; it is obviously an attempt to attribute
certain fixed habits to the stock market **and**
operate on these habits. But the habits of the
market are erratic and conditions are constantly
changing. The intermediate fluctuations of a

few points usually represent nothing more important than the needs of day-to-day speculators or the plans of unimportant manipulators. The stop loss order, and all the other mechanical devices would work excellently if the market were a machine with fixed perennial movements—but it is not.

In a majority of instances the stop loss orders are reached. That is to say if a purchase is made at 100 accompanied by an order to stop the loss at 98, the order will be executed more often than not. The very existence of stop loss orders in volume often causes a decline which will catch them. So popular has the use of this mischievous method become that the bears are always on the alert to "go gunning for stops." A recent glaring instance of this was on the morning following the American Tobacco decision by the Supreme Court. Prices had been advancing and hundreds of orders were placed to "stop losses" two or three points below the opening level. A concentrated drive by the bears did the work in an hour or two; the stop loss orders were caught and the market resumed its advancing trend and reached the highest prices of the year a day or two later. The stop loss exponents simply created a condition which drove them out of the market at the lowest prices.

It is the pet theory of the stop loss people that the market will naturally swing *below* their stop and so enable them to repurchase at a lower level. If a man could buy at 100, sell at 98 and repurchase at 96, there would be an advantage, but there is no good reason to expect that this will happen. The basic theory of mechanical market devices is the same as that of any other gambling machine and the calculus of probabilities would apply in the same manner. I have in the past prepared extensive figures which show that so far as precedent can enlighten us, there is no more reason for expecting one ten-point decline than five two-point declines and that therefore nothing is gained by the use of stop orders.

But let me now expose the greatest fallacy of all. The makers of tables and charts demonstrating the possibilities of the stop loss order as a basis of speculative ventures almost invariably assume that purchases and sales can be made at certain fixed prices. They show how, in the past performances of the market, an order to buy might have been placed above the market at say 102 when the price was 100 and that the security then advanced to 105 and could have been sold at that price with a three-point profit. They further demonstrate that in many cases where the stop was placed on the original trade an advantage could be gained by repurchasing lower than the stop. For example a purchase is made at 100, with an order to sell at 98. The price declines to 96, and the stock is repurchased—advantage 2 points. This looks very well on paper, but there is absolutely no guarantee that these orders *can* be filled according to the program. The assumption that they can is wholly unwarranted in all cases. The first order to buy at 102 when the market was 100 might or might not be executed. A rapidly advancing market might skip the fixed limit entirely, sales showing at say 101½ and 102½ with no intermediate transactions at 102. Sometimes the order is placed at "102 or higher," in which case the stock might be purchased at 102½. I say "might" because even if the fixed price is touched, there might be orders for 1,000 shares at that price and only 100 shares for sale, so that only one-tenth of the orders could be filled.

The stop loss order placed with the original purchase is even more unsafe, as there are more possibilities of rapid and sensational declines than advances. A rising market is more or less orderly as compared with a declining market. An accident cannot bring about a ten-point general advance over night, but it can and sometimes dose bring about a ten-point decline. Suppose a purchase is made at 100 accompanied by a stop at 98 and an order to repurchase at 96—there is no guarantee that any of these things will be done. The original price of 100 may be touched with so little stock for sale that the market recovers without the order being filled. If it is filled at 100 the decline may be so rapid that the stop loss order to sell cannot be executed above 97, even if 98 is touched on the way down. If the two first orders are satisfactorily executed, and the market declines to 96, it may or may not be possible to repurchase at that price. More serious still is the situation where a purchase is made at, say 100, with a stop order to sell at 98, and the market for the stock opens off, say 10 points the next morning. In this case the stop order would be filled at 90, and a sacrifice of the stock would follow at what would probably be nearly the bottom price. This is what happened to hundreds of people the morning after R. P. Flower's death, and in many other instances.

The exponents of stop loss orders will say that I am quoting exceptions and that in a majority of cases orders will be satisfactorily executed. Granted—but these things happen often enough in a year's trading to completely destroy their pictured or tabulated exhibits, and to turn their theoretical profits into actual losses.

In the foregoing statement a fixed mechanical rule has been assumed and no mention made of the mental drawbacks. If a stop loss order could be placed at 98 on a purchase made at 100, and a 'repurchase effected at 96, all well and good; but how often the purchaser becomes disturbed and confused by the spectacle of rapidly declining prices and fails to carry out his plans. The market always "looks weak" when it is declining, and declines are always accompanied by wild stories and predictions which are usually the result of the decline rather than the cause of it. It is cold comfort to see a stop order executed at 98 and in a few days find the market much higher with no stock on hand. The "stop loss" order has proven to be a "make loss" order.

Contrast the results of the scale order as applied to the above illustration. Scale orders are not always executed when the limits are barely touched, but in case of a heavy decline over night there is an advantage instead of a drawback, as the intended line is purchased at a lower level than was originally contemplated. The scale order properly used, seldom results in failure. If we are satisfied in the first place that the security purchased is cheap, and the prospects good, a decline is an advantage instead of a disaster.

Speculators would be better off if all the mechanical methods in existence had never been invented.

CHAPTER X.

Mental Characteristics.

It appears strange that the mental characteristics of speculators or investors should be a continual source of needless worry and actual loss, but the fact that it is so, is incontrovertible.

The mental attitude of speculators during panic periods is responsible for about as much loss, in a negative sense of the word, as is the lack of funds. People who see great bargains littering the Wall Street counters, and who have every reason to know that they are bargains, become confused and frightened by the declining prices, the bank failures and the words of pessimists, and fail to take advantage of unprecedented or unusual opportunities. They become obsessed with the idea that the whole business structure is going to pieces; that the mills, factories and railroads will cease to operate, and they look back through history for the worst precedents they can find and draw comparisons regardless of the fact that basic factors may be entirely different. It is a well-known fact that public venturers or investors seldom buy near the bottom. The stocks are accumulated by the wise minority at such times and are resold to the public later on at much higher prices. Per contra, when prices are high and business is booming, there is a spirit of mental exhilaration in the air and ill-advised purchases are numerous.

So strong is the human tendency to become depressed when prices of securities are depressed, and to become stimulated when prices are high, that the majority of operators find it impossible

to carry out their preconceived plans, no matter
how reasonable and correct such plans may be.
An individual, looking over the history of security movements, will sometimes make up his mind
quite correctly that in every period of panic won-
derful opportunities occur in the securities markets and that when business is good and prices
are high, we may expect another reversal sooner
or later. Realizing all this, he makes up his mind
to await such an opportunity—to buy when no
one else wants to buy and sell when no one else
wants to sell. A very wise plan. But when he
is confronted by the actual conditions for which
he has waited, he will in nine cases out of ten
abandon his plans.

And this indecision is not confined to the long
swing operators. It is even more prevalent and
pronounced in the case of active speculators or
investors who enter the market frequently. Sev-
enty-five per cent of the orders placed by speculators to buy or sell if certain prices are reached,
are cancelled whenever the market approaches
their prices. Let me again refer to the recent
American Tobacco decision as an illustration of
this propensity. In the few weeks preceding that
decision there were marked evidences of basic
improvement in the general situation. Crop prospects were excellent, and the only bar to advancing prices was the uncertainty over the Supreme
Court's construction of the Sherman law. A great
many people reasoned about as follows:

If the construction placed on the Sherman law
in this case is not revolutionary and confiscatory,
the uncertainty will be removed, and even if the
American Tobacco Company is found guilty,
good corporations will not suffer. Fundamental
conditions are such that we should have a better

market and higher stock prices. If the decision is against the company we may expect an initial decline of a few points, as the purport of the decision will not be fully understood at once, and some frightened selling will ensue. On such a decline, stocks will be an excellent purchase. That is the way they reasoned and they were absolutely right. A great many orders to buy a few points under the market were placed with brokers. The next morning the market began rapidly declining and many of these buying limits were reached But at the first sign of demoralization marketwise, cancellations began pouring in and only a small percentage of the orders was executed. In short, these people figured out what might naturally be expected to happen, and how it might be used to the greatest advantage; that very thing did happen exactly as expected, and they would have none of it. This kind of vacillation is very bad. It is largely due to too close attention to the ticker. Ordinary fluctuations are greatly magnified in importance when every little change is watched. As has been stated, the market always "looks weak" when it is declining, and "looks strong" when it is advancing. Consequently it alternately looks weak or strong half a dozen times a day. Propinquity of this character is seldom an advantage except to professional scalpers, and is a fertile source of confusion and loss to the rank and file.

It is the same way with the scale order. A man makes up his mind that a security is cheap and that its prospects are bright. He wishes to make some allowance for errors in calculation or natural market action, so he decides to introduce a scale order, to buy say every two points down until his intended line is accumulated. Now the only way the full line can be accumulated is by a decline. That is the basic theory of the method, and a decline is necessary and desirable. If we start buying on a scale at, say, 100, with orders to buy at 98, 96, 94, 92 and 90, and these orders are all filled, the average price would be 95 for the entire line. When the price returns to the original point (100) there is a five-point profit, while if the whole had been purchased at 100, no profit would be shown. But knowing and appreciating all this, the plan mapped out originally is seldom pursued to a conclusion. The spectacle of falling prices (which were anticipated as being possible or probable, and also desirable) is too much for the venturer. He cancels his orders in the fear that the bottom will fall out of the market or he doubles his purchases in the belief that he will not get his desired line. If the market advances from the original purchase he is not contented to reflect that he has acted in the interests of safety and to be thankful for moderate gains, but is incensed because he has not made more, and this often leads to increasing purchases on an advance which is just the reverse of what he set out to do.

Speculators and investors are almost certain to exaggerate the importance of events or news items bearing on security prices, and on the other hand to ignore or underestimate the importance of fundamental factors. The development of basic conditions is slow and requires constant attention, therefore the study is usually neglected.

If the dividend on a security is reduced or passed for any reason, we are bound to hear predictions of similar forthcoming reductions in many quarters. The action may be for a specific reason in no way affecting other securities or may be a good business move, but that does not matter to the traders. They do not stop to analyze or segregate the case. Visions of wholesale reductions appear, and the visions are soon converted into verbal expressions of opinion; the verbal utterances grow into predictions and predictions develop into "information." A dividend reduction for a good and specific reason affecting no other corporation usually winds up inside of twenty-four hours in "We hear on good authority" statements attacking the stability of other corporations.

In reading crop reports, earnings, statements or whatever, this same slipshod superficial reasoning or apprehension is constantly in evidence. The only way this evil influence can be avoided is by keeping so well posted that we may know what to expect or be able to intelligently weigh the purport of unexpected news. A day's market gossip would fill a volume, and all that is of value in it would not ordinarily fill a page.

Political issues are constantly made a source of agitation and worry in the speculative world. In nine cases out of ten the results of important changes in laws or methods are beneficial to the country as a whole and to the stockholder or speculator. It is hard to find a flaw in the actions of the Interstate Commerce Commission since that body was organized. We have better and more uniform reports of railway earnings and operations than ever before, and the only time the railroads have been refused a request, it has been found that such request was unreasonable or that the necessity for the demands was misrepresented. It did appear a few years ago that with the prices of commodities and labor advancing

without corresponding advances in the price of
transportation, the railroads were in a bad position, but when it came down to an actual test of
the facts as brought out by the recent rate case,
it was shown that the only material increase was
in the cost of labor, and that materials used in
construction and price were in most cases lower
than in the past. Great savings had also been
effected through increased car and train load ca-
pacity, improved grades and more efficient management. The railroads made a strong case, but
it was not strong enough. After all was said and
done it was found that they were in a better general position than at any time in history, and
that the return on railroad securities was larger,
dollar for dollar, than it had ever been before.
Therefore, the demands were justly refused. We
may be sure that if the time ever comes when
an advance in rates is necessary to a fair return
on investments, the advance will be granted.

There is always some kind of political agitation
going on and when a decline in securities or general business occurs, it is popular to attribute it
to politics. A case in point was the panic of 1907.
People who did not foresee or recognize the over-
strained credit conditions, our extravagance, and
a dozen other fundamental factors which brought
about that panic, cast about for something tangible on which to lay the blame. They found it in
the political agitation. Such agitation had been
going on for years and had no power to either
make or prevent the crash of 1907. It is true
that unwise ranting somewhat aggravated the
trouble in its last stages, as such strictures were
ill-timed and increased the apprehension of a mul-
titude which was already badly frightened, but
this was at best only a contributory reason, even

as applied to the final spasm. The last throes of the panic were due more to money conditions than to anything else.

It is only when some great issue is pending that politics have power to radically change the natural course of security prices for any length of time. The silver agitation was a serious factor marketwise, but it is questionable if another such issue will ever be presented. The tariff is the bugaboo at present, but a radical change in this regard would have a very mixed effect on security values and prices, and would not precipitate a panic. Some corporations would be injured, others would be benefited and we are bound to assume until it is otherwise proven by a sufficient lapse of time, that tariff changes would be beneficial to the country as a whole, and consequently to its security issues.

Every year we raise a crop of agitators, some honest and correct in their views and some working only for political advancement or aggrandizement, regardless of the merits of their propaganda. The latter come to Washington, squib off their verbal firecrackers for the edification of prejudiced or unthinking constituents; get their fulminations spread on the records and go home. They do no harm, so far as the market for securities is concerned. We have had them with us since the constitution was signed and we will always have them with ps. They are harmless, but they are disconcerting to the timid public investors or speculators. If they had never existed, or had existed in greater numbers for the last twenty years, the average level of security prices would in all probability not be appreciably different from what it is today.

Of the numerous mental failings, it is probable

that greed is the most prolific mother of loss. It leads to over-speculation, to rash operations regardless of the merits of securities, and to dissatisfaction with what has been gained. In regard to the latter phase of the question, it is rather astonishing to see a man pocketing a profit which would have been considered very large, considering time and capital employed, in any other business on earth, cursing his stars fluently because he did not make more. It is very easy to look back on the *possibilities* after it is all over and indulge in retrospective speculation, but these tentative operations could never have been undertaken if the factor of safety had been properly conserved and such retrospects are chimerical. They are about as reasonable and about as productive of profit as looking back over the records of numbers established in a game of roulette and figuring how much would have been won by betting on all of them. This mental state has one bad effect. It encourages people to over-reach themselves in future operations and so eventually becomes productive of loss.

There are many other fallacious mental characteristics which retard, disturb and mislead the speculator and investor, but a remedy for these drawbacks may all be covered in one prescription. Make up your mind what you are going to do and why you are going to do it. Be sure your original premises are correct; keep posted as to changes or developments; pay no heed to fluctuations or "tips." Disregard every bit of gossip masquerading as news, except what is genuinely informative and based on good authority; do not be moved from your position by canards, incompetent advice or anything else short of an actual change in the conditions on which your actions were originally based; be satisfied with reasonable returns, and learn to accept a loss quickly if your plans are upset by miscalculations or adverse developments; and remember that the market, with fresh opportunities, will be doing business at the same old stand tomorrow, and next week, and next year.

CHAPTER XI.

The Future of Our Railroad and Industrial Securities.

The long future of our securities is a question of great importance to the speculator as well as the investor. Even if we are operating only for the shorter turns of a year or less, it is a distinct advantage to be working with the current instead of against it. If a man buys a security with a well based opinion that it will eventually be worth more than its present selling price and is disappointed in the immediate movement of the stock, he can rest easy in the knowledge that at some time in the future his profits will appear. Intermediate paper losses do not seriously affect him unless he has committed the sin of over-speculation.

The progress of some of our leading railroad stocks in the past two decades reads like a Golconda romance. Atchison, Topeka & Santa Fe sold under foreclosure in 1895 at $3.50 per share; Baltimore & Ohio in the same year at $32.50 per share; Canadian Pacific at $33 per share; Jersey Central at $81.50; Chesapeake & Ohio at $12.50 per share; C., B, & Q. at $69 per share; Chicago, Milwaukee & St. Paul at $53.87 per share; Chicago & Northwestern at $87.37 per share; Louisville & Nashville at $39; Northern Pacific at $2.50 per share; Reading at $15 per share; Southern Pacific at $16.75 per share; Union Pacific at $4 per share, and so on through a long line of others. It may be suggested that this was in a period of panic and unusual opportunities, which is true enough, but if we go back only one decade and consult the progress since that time, the presentation is still remarkable. Prices of the stocks named above were as follows in the year 1900: Atchison, $18.62; Baltimore & Ohio, $55.25; Canadian Pacific, $84.75; Jersey Central, $115; Chesapeake & Ohio, $24; Chicago, Burlington & Quincy, $119; Chicago, Milwaukee & St. Paul, $108.50; Chicago & Northwestern, $157.50; Louisville & Nashville, $68.25; Northern Pacific, $45.75; Reading, $15; Southern Pacific, $30.37, and Union Pacific, $44.37.

In calling attention to this remarkable growth in an address delivered before the Finance Forum of New York in 1910, I was asked by a gentleman in the audience if, in my opinion, such opportunities existed today or would ever exist again. I had no hesitation in replying in the affirmative. It goes without saying that the opportunities shown in the stocks mentioned will never be presented again, but some of our railroad stocks which are now kicking about the street paying no dividends will in the fullness of time duplicate the performances of what are now known as our gilt-edged railroad stocks. The bold statement that such stocks as Erie, Missouri Pacific, *et al,* will in time sell as high as Union Pacific or Great Northern would be more likely to be met with ridicule than with respectful attention, but in that regard it may be pointed out that the man who ten or fifteen years ago had predicted the present prices of Union Pacific, Atchison or Great Northern, would doubtless have been considered a subject for an *inquirendo lunatico.* With the steady growth in population, the increased efficiency and improved management of railroad properties, we may expect to see many securities which are now despised taking front rank in the speculative list. Meanwhile our present market leaders will have become seasoned investments and will have practically passed from the street, as has been the case with Delaware & Lackawanna, Chicago & Northwestern and other erstwhile active stocks.

We cannot learn much about this long swing of prices from an examination of statistical exhibits. The statistical condition of Atchison or Union Pacific could not have been very hopeful when they were sold under the hammer. What must be depended on is the long future of the territory traversed. We may, however, obtain help from statistics in choosing our prospective bargains by watching the course of improvement in financing and managing, and so make the original purchases under promising conditions and prospects.

Taking up first the long future of our railroads as a whole, we find much that is very encouraging. Let us examine a few of the salient points. The principal bugaboo at present is the cry of over-capitaliation. Considered as a whole, our railroads are not over-capitalized. Recent attempts at physical valuation by certain states have gone far toward establishing that fact. The so-called physical valuation made by Texas and Michigan may be cast aside as worthless. No statistician of ability would accept their figures seriously. The Texas valuation was based on the year 1895, which in itself is sufficient to damn it. No pretence of thoroughness is shown in the Michigan figures of 1900. Aside from these, the physical valuation made by the State of Washington in 1905 gives the cost of reproducing railroads in that State at $194,000,000 (in round numbers); the present value at $176,-000,000 and capitalization at $167,000,000. Minnesota in 1907 gave cost of reproduction at $412,-000,000; value at $360,000,000 and capitalization $335,000,000. Wisconsin in 1909 gave cost of reproduction $297,000,000; value $241,000,000 and capitalization $249,000,000. South Dakota in 1908 gave cost of reproduction $106,000,000; value $92,000,000 and capitalization $139,000,000. Professor Dixon of the Bureau of Railway Economics at Washington threw out the Texas report as worthless and reduced the Minnesota capitalization to $300,000,000 because of obvious duplications. South Dakota also showed duplications by including a share in terminals at St. Paul and Chicago. Subtracting these, the South Dakota capitalization would be $109,000,000 instead of $139,000,000. The Wisconsin board included in their physical valuation about $25,-000,000 of the Chicago, Milwaukee & St. Paul's investment in the Chicago, Milwaukee & Puget Sound extension, which had already been charged to other States. Deducting this, the Wisconsin figures would be $224,000,000 instead of $249,-000,000.

An examination of these estimates made by detached States shows so many duplications and errors of calculation that the whole affair is a jumble of incoherent figures, which are naturally biased in order to increase state taxation. The only way we will ever arrive at a reasonable physical valuation is to have the Government take the matter up and perform the work uniformly and scientifically.

By comparison with foreign countries our capitalization per mile is very low. The railroads of the United Kingdom show capitalization of $274,-964 per mile; Germany, $111,737 per mile; Russia, $79,136 per mile; France, $141,920 per mile;

Austria, $115,130 per mile, and Italy, $125,205 per mile. The per mile capitalization of all European roads averages $126,859 per mile of line. This would be considerably decreased by figuring on per mile of track, as the United Kingdom has more than twice as many miles of track as miles of line, while the United States has only about one-third more, but figuring any way we please and making all allowances, the railroad capitalization of the United States, which is $58,316 per mile of line and $40,860 per mile of track, is very low as compared with other countries. Even our next door neighbor, Canada, has a per mile capitalization of $64,740.

In the last decade the net capitalization per mile of line of all railroads in the United States has increased a trifle over 14% (not 14% per annum, but for the entire period). In the same time net earnings per mile have increased 43.7% and the ratio of expenses to earnings has increased 2.2%. The average tons to the train load has increased in the ten years 40.9%. The larger train loads are a great economical measure and go a long way toward offsetting the higher compensation paid employees. According to the railroad statistics offered for popular consumption, the compensation paid to employees has increased 103% in the last decade, but this statement has been frequently so presented as to lead to the opinion that it means that wages have doubled, which is far from being the truth. The joker is in the omission of the word "all." What is really shown is that the amount of money paid to a greatly increased number of employees has increased 103%. In the decade, the number of employees per mile has increased 38.5%. Whatever the railroads may claim about the cost of running railroads ten years ago as compared with today, they cannot get behind the fact that the ratio of expenses to earnings has only increased 2.2% in ten years or at the rate of 0.22% per annum. And it may be said in passing that much of this increase is probably due to bookkeeping, as it is impossible to prevent accountants from charging to maintenance items that should be charged to improvements or new construction and so pass into capital account. If, for example, ten miles of track is washed away and is rebuilt on a new grade over new ground, the railroad can charge it to replacement or new construction according to their own sweet will. It does not seem reasonable to assume that in the recent efforts to make a bad mouth the railroads would fail to take advantage of this method of accounting so far as possible.

In the above figures of increase in ratio of operating expenses, I have taken the figures offered by the railroads themselves in the seventh annual statistical number of the *Bureau of Railway News and Statistics.* They do not square with the figures given by independent statisticians. *Poor's Manual* gives the ratio of expenses to earnings in 1901 as 68.93 and in 1910 as 66.09. The figures given by the railroads of percentage earned on net capitalization are also confusing and misleading so far as the progress of stock securities is concerned. They bulk all capitalization, bonds, notes and stocks, and show that they are earning no more on net capitalization than they were 20 years ago. But when we examine these figures in detail, we find that the interest rate has fallen rapidly in that period while the dividend rate has been rising. This may not please the buyer of bonds, but certainly the holder of stock securities can find no fault with such re-adjustment. Over half the total capitalization of our railroads is in the bonded debt, and it is obviously to the advantage of all concerned to borrow such capital cheaply. Here are the figures for twenty-eight years as given by *Poor's Manual*:

Table Showing Average Rate Per Cent. of Interest and Dividends on Bonds and Stocks of All United States Railroads—1883 to 1910 Inclusive.

Year	Interest Aver. rate %	Dividends Aver. rate %	Year	Interest Aver. rate %	Dividends Aver. rate %
1883	4.94	2.76	1897	4.24	1.51
1884	4.82	2.50	1898	4.21	1.71
1885	4.97	2.00	1899	4.26	1.92
1886	4.86	2.02	1900	4.27	2.44
1887	4.86	2.17	1901	4.24	2.65
1888	4.48	1.80	1902	4.10	2.97
1889	4.53	1.79	1903	4.17	3.03
1890	4.44	1.82	1904	4.01	3.31
1891	4.41	1.87	1905	3.79	3.27
1892	4.25	1.93	1906	3.99	3.63
1893	4.31	1.88	1907	3.87	3.73
1894	4.19	1.66	1908	3.88	3.50
1895	4.24	1.58	1909	3.87	3.68
1896	4.45	1.52	1910	3.79	3.64

While we are not nearing the end of railroad construction in the United States, the building of new lines and opening up of new territory will not be so rapid from now on. This will greatly enhance the value of the existing roads, particularly those traversing the least developed and most sparsely populated territory, that is to say, the Northwest and Southwest. The roads covering such territory have been called on to spend enormous sums in reducing grades, shortening routes and improving roadbeds and terminals. As population increases we will find from now on that a great deal of the increased demand for transportation facilities will be provided by double tracking, and double tracking is the most profitable of all railway construction. It will be a long time before any great amount of new trunk line construction will be necessary. Of course the growth and prosperity of Western roads will materially increase the traffic and earnings of Eastern lines, but the greatest benefit will accrue to properties of the Northwest and Southwest.

The future of our industrial securities is not so clear as that of the railroads. They are a mixed lot, and, as a group, are comparatively new. They are also comparatively low in price. The greatest reason given for avoiding industrial securities is the fear of tariff changes or hostile legislation. Personally, I do not think this apprehension is well founded. The laws will eventually drive evil out of corporate combinations of capital, and in so far as a corporation has been gaining by corrupt or high-handed practices, it will suffer. Also, when a corporation thrives because of a ridiculously high tariff, its future is endangered, but there is no necessity for choosing securities whose prosperity is based on such temporary emoluments. There are plenty of good industrial stocks with clean records and bright prospects. Most of the industrial preferred securities have excellent dividend records and are the cheapest of all semi-investment stocks. It is not the purpose, in this chapter, to offer specific recommendations, as changes might occur at any time to warrant a modification or reversal of opinion, but an examination of the reports and statistics of some of the oldest industrials will show that they have greatly enriched their holders and maintained dividends in the face of legislative attacks, or even when moderately affected by tariff changes. In its incipient stages every new industrial security has passed through a baptism of fire and large numbers of people who want something new and who brush aside opportunities in the seasoned securities in the same group, in order to get in on the ground floor of a new flotation, are crippled by their actions. They usually get in on the roof and fall off. A large combination is usually over-capitalized at the start, as it is necessary to pay fancy prices for the competitive properties purchased. Many properties so purchased are in a poor physical state, and much money is necessary to bring them up to the standard. The management is also in a more or less confused state at first, and the whole combination, while it may be theoretically correct, is in an embryo state. I regret to add that in many cases the promoters take advantage of the public tendency referred to and sell them stock at prices which are too high. In the course of time, the over-capitalization is absorbed, the plants are up to date, the managerial machinery is well oiled and the stocks, disgorged by the disgusted public, are low in price. At such a time industrial stocks present great speculative opportunities, but the same public which was so enthusiastic at the beginning will not accept them as a gift. We can look back over the statistical records of the past decade and find dozens of such cases, not differing in any way from the hypothesis offered above.

One drawback to operations in industrial securities is the lack of comprehensiveness and uniformity in their published reports. Some of them are mere balance sheets and tell little or nothing. Some of the larger corporations, however, are publishing annual reports which are as clear and complete as any railroad report. It is to be hoped that other corporations whose stocks are held by the public will see fit to accept such documents as models and reform their methods of publicity and accounting. Failing in this it is to be hoped they will be required to do so by our law-makers as was the case with the railroads. Probably nothing would contribute to a speedy reform in this direction so much as a refusal on the part of the public to participate in blind pool flotations. It is good policy to take that stand at any rate. A stockholder is entitled to full knowledge of the undertaking in which he is a partner and there can be no reasons for concealment except ulterior ones.

In a few years some of the industrial preferred stocks which now show a large income return will pass into the hands of investors at materially higher prices. When confidence in the stability of their dividends is assured such securities should sell on a basis to yield about 5%. A seven per cent. preferred industrial stock, of which there are a number, would be on a five per cent. basis selling at $140 per share. There is a maxim in financial circles that an industrial security should pay a higher return on money than a railroad security, but this should not apply to preferences with a large margin of safety. The fluctuations in dividends on common stocks are more frequent than on the preferences and in many cases the dividends on preferred issues are "cumulative," that is to say, all deferred dividends must be made up to the holders of preferred before the common issues receive anything.

Another point in favor of the industrial stocks of both classes is the very small percentage of bonded indebtedness. This permits them to go through lean periods more easily than railroads or other corporations having heavy fixed charges, and gives an added book value to the junior issues.

The desires and intentions of different people and the specific influences bearing on different securities render it impossible to lay down a rule of thumb as to just what should be purchased for the most satisfactory results. A rough formula which will cover most cases would be about as follows:

For the most stable income with chances of moderate appreciation in value, the high priced rails having a good dividend record covering a long period of years, a low ratio of expenses to earnings and low fixed charges.

For a somewhat larger income return and better chances of ultimate appreciation in value, but with less safety, the industrial preferred stocks having a good dividend record. Choose the stocks which are not likely to be seriously affected by legislation or tariff changes. To this group, I would add the common stocks of public utility corporations, gas, electric lighting and water. The traction group is not so good, particularly the securities of urban traction lines, as they find it very difficult to keep down expenses or advance fares and are constantly getting into litigation.

For greater speculative chances, with the safety of income reduced, the middle priced railroad common stocks which show low fixed charges, good management and a brilliant future from territorial expansion. This group, which is comprised mainly of Northwestern and Southwestern roads, presents, in my opinion, the greatest speculative promise, together with the greatest certainty of future income return.

For speculative chances regardless of income or immediate dividend returns, the low priced rails, particularly such as are low in price because of bad management, bad financing, etc., but which have good future possibilities through territorial expansion. Whether we buy one of these low priced railroad stocks for any of the reasons given or for all of them, statistics will not help us much. They will be the best bargains when their statistical exhibits are the worst. We must depend on improved management and financing and natural growth. It is reasonable to assume that when a good property or group of properties is neglected or mismanaged for years, something will be done to rectify these conditions. If nothing is done voluntarily, it will be done automatically by a receivership. The reader will instantly revert to one group of properties in reading the above paragraph, so I will not need to name it.

The low priced industrial common stocks may also be considered as offering great speculative opportunities. It is necessary to employ unusual discrimination in choosing these issues. In some cases the business of industrial corporations fluctuates so tremendously that dividends are never assured for any length of time. It is a common, and frequently a fatal error to look at the earnings and progress of a year or two and form conclusions accordingly.

CHAPTER XII.

Speculation in Commodities.

The amount of money lost in speculation in commodities has been much greater proportionately than that lost in securities. An exhaustive examination of 500 speculative accounts operated in the years 1901, 1902 and 1903 revealed 412 commodity accounts that showed a loss; 74 a profit and 14 were neutral. This would be very much changed for the better by an examination of an equal number of accounts covering any period during the last five years. There are two reasons for this—first, that the trend of all speculative commodity prices has been upward, and, as the public operates on the long side in a majority of cases, they would have been favored in their ventures. Second, and more important, is the fact that a number of shrewd men have arrived at a somewhat tardy recognition of a gradual but steady advance in the prices of commodities which continually shifts the *normal* price to a higher basis. They realize that a price for wheat, corn or cotton which would have appeared high a few years ago is low now. Prior to the recognition of this upward trend they were floundering around in the dark and drawing wholly incorrect comparisons and deductions. They did not know when wheat or corn or cotton was cheap or when it was dear. Furthermore, the cause of this gradual readjustment of prices to a higher level was not understood, and consequently they did not know when it would cease, or when the trend might be reversed. This finally led to the only reasonable method of solving the problem, i.e., an assiduous search for the *cause* of the change. After this study had been brought to a satisfactory conclusion, it changed the whole aspect of commodity speculation, and more fortunes have been made and retained in cereal and cotton speculation in the last five years than at any time in history. It is needless to state that the important operators who worked on that theory did not advertise it from the housetops. They did not in any way relax their investigations as to crop prospects, exports or any of the other factors bearing on intermediate price changes, but in addition to the advantages of such knowledge they operated on a *law* governing the long swing of prices, and this enabled them to swim with the current at all times. If their deductions as to crop prospects or supply and demand were incorrect and their operations proved temporarily disastrous, they could maintain their position until the natural course of prices to a higher level had overcome the errors of judgment.

Again, a recognition of the trend will permit us to make allowances for it in consulting precedents. Many people have been ruined by selling commodities because statistics showed the price to be high and that much lower prices had been established under certain conditions in the past. Finding the same conditions today in the way of supply and demand, crop prospects, etc., as obtained in a former year, the speculator cannot always see why equally low prices should not be made. If everything was equal he would be right, but everything is not equal.

Let us see if we cannot clear this point up and establish a rough working basis.

It is a matter of common knowledge that prices

of commodities generally have been rising for
years with occasional reactions in periods of hard
times or following panic periods. The Gibson
index number shows the following changes since
1900:

GIBSON'S INDEX NUMBERS.
(Showing cost of living)

Year	All foods	Clothing	Minerals	Other	All other than foods	Total
1890 . .	43.4	17.3	15.5	15.4	48.3	91.6
1895 . .	42.0	15.3	11.0	13.2	39.5	81.5
1900 . .	44.2	16.3	14.8	16.1	47.2	91.4
1905 . .	47.3	18.0	16.0	17.1	51.0	98.3
1906 . .	49.8	19.2	16.6	19.6	55.4	105.2
1907 . .	50.9	20.8	18.9	19.3	59.0	109.9
1908 . .	54.2	17.6	15.4	18.3	51.3	105.5
1909 . .	59.2	17.3	15.2	20.2	52.7	111.9
1910 . .	59.3	18.9	15.4	21.6	55.9	115.2
1911.						
Jan. . .	54.3	19.5	15.2	19.9	54.6	108.9
Feb. . .	52.9	19.1	15.1	20.1	54.3	107.3
Mar. . .	53.3	18.9	15.1	20.2	54.2	107.5
Apr. . .	53.1	18.8	14.9	19.4	53.1	106.2
May . .	53.5	19.1	14.8	19.2	53.1	106.5
June . .	52.9	19.0	14.8	19.1	52.9	105.8
July . .	57.5	18.4	14.8	19.3	52.5	110.0
Aug. . .	60.1	17.5	14.8	19.1	51.4	111.5
Sept. . .	61.2	17.1	14.7	19.7	51.5	112.9
Oct. . .	62.0	16.7	14.5	19.4	50.5	112.5
Nov. . .	61.3	16.2	14.5	18.9	49.5	110.8
Dec. . .	60.8	16.0	14.8	18.5	49.3	110.1

It will be observed that the price of foodstuffs
has advanced since 1900 from 44.2 to 60.8.
Downward fluctuations occur at times, but the declines have been in the nature of reactions and,
unless the influence which is causing the advancing prices ceases or is reversed, we may expect
this trend to continue upward. As to what that
cause is, I will speak later.

Now let us see how this has been reflected in the prices of wheat, corn and oats. In order to determine this it will be necessary to arrive at an average price for each year. To take merely the high and low of the year and accept the middle point would not give a very sound showing, so I have taken the high and low for each month of each year and averaged the whole twelve months. The results are as follows:

Average Cash Prices of Wheat, Corn and Oats
(1900 to 1910 inclusive)

Year.	Wheat.	Corn.	Oats.
1900	$ .71	$ .38	$ .22½
1901	.72	.49½	.32
1902	.72½	.59½	.37
1903	.79½	.46	.35½
1904	1.03½	.50½	.37
1905	1.01	.50	.30
1906	.79½	.46	.32½
1907	.91	.53	.45
1908	.97½	.68½	.50½
1909	1.20½	.66½	.48
1910	1.10	.58	.38½

Allowing for all the influences of large or small crops, it is evident that there is a decided upward trend to prices. A year of abnormally large production following a previous big year will bring the price level down materially, but the trend upward is soon resumed. 1906 is an example of this.

Taking the last five years as a basis and throwing off 20 cents a bushel on the average price established in 1909, which was artificially too high, we find that the average price of wheat has been above 95 cents, corn above 58 cents and the average price of oats about 43 cents. Allowing for the fact that this average covers a five-year period and that the trend has been upward from year to year, barring temporary reversals, it is safe to say that the nominal price of wheat under normal conditions is about $1, corn about 62 cents and oats about 45 cents. Of course higher or lower prices are established from year to year. These movements give us the speculative opportunities we are looking for.

In cotton we find that the upward trend has been even more pronounced. This is partly due to the fact that in addition to the natural forces making for a higher level in prices of commodities, production of cotton is not keeping pace with increased consumption. The progress of prices during the last ten years has been as follows:

Average Price of Cotton.

(Seasons of 1900 to 1910 inclusive)

1900-01........ 7.89 cents per pound
1901-02........ 7.40   "   "   "
1902-03........ 9.99   "   "   "
1903-04........12.42   "   "   "
1904-05........ 8.66   "   "   "
1905-06........10.83   "   "   "
1906-07........10.68   "   "   "
1907-08........11.11   "   ..   ..
1908-09........10.01   "   "   "
1909-10........14.45   "   "   "

Eliminating artificial prices made temporarily in 1903-04 and 1909-10, and allowing for increase due to natural causes and the excess of demand over production, we may reasonably fix the nominal price of cotton at about 12 cents per pound.

The greatest opportunities in commodity speculation come at such times as prices are unduly depressed because of large supplies or good crop prospects, or through manipulative tactics. Occasionally it is possible to buy wheat at 75 or 80 cents a bushel, corn at 40 or 45 cents per bushel, oats around 30 cents per bushel, and cotton around 9 cents per pound. Purchases made at such prices are almost certain to bring handsome profits in a reasonable length of time, regardless of what conditions may be at the time of purchase. Of course conditions will frequently make it inadvisable to wait for such low prices as this, but when they do appear they may be used as a confident basis of purchases.

Under normal conditions, with crop prospects fair, supplies on hand about an average and exports keeping along at about the usual pace, it is safe to buy wheat around 90 cents, corn around 50 cents and cotton below 12 cents. Such purchases will almost certainly turn out well if patience is exercised.

The scale order method is well adapted to trading in commodities, as fluctuations are wider and more frequent than in stocks, and the means of computing values of grain or cotton are not so extensive or accurate as in securities.

As stated heretofore, in deciding as to the probability of this upward trend being continued, we must first determine the cause that has brought about the higher prices during the past decade or more. Several theories have been advanced by economists, but all have been found faulty or unconvincing except one—the increasing gold supply of the world. A majority of the earnest students of the subject have adopted this theory, some of them quickly and others grudgingly. Not only is the consensus of competent opinion in favor of the theory, but the few writers and thinkers who promulgated it years ago have proven their case by correct predictions of what might be expected to happen to the prices of both securities and commodities, so long as the increasing supply of gold continues. These writers, for example, contended that securities having a fixed rate of interest must fall in price unless the rate of interest was advanced. They did not except such premier investment securities as British Consols. They contended that the price of commodities generally would continue to rise. Both these things have happened just as was predicted. There have been temporary reversals, of course, but these proved to be fluctuations and nothing more.

The theory of the increasing gold supply and its effect on prices cannot here be discussed in detail. There are many ramifications and offshoots, and a comprehensive discussion of the subject would require a volume in itself. Simply stated, the theory is as follows:

The world's gold supply has continued to increase more rapidly than population for years. It is an inexorable law of supply and demand that when any commodity is over-produced it must fall in price. Gold, being a fixed standard, cannot fall in actual figures, but it does fall through a rise in the prices of the things for which gold can be exchanged. The reason bonds fall in price is that when capital invested in bonds is returned at the maturity of the issue, the purchasing power of that capital has been impaired. It will not buy so much food or machinery or clothing. We have no way to measure the value of money except by its purchasing power. Commodities rise in price because gold cannot fall in price, although it can and does in value. It appears to me idle to attempt to refute the statement that an oversupply of gold will necessarily advance the price of all that gold will buy. Let us assume, for the sake of argument, that to-morrow a mountain of pure gold is discovered containing ten times as much of the metal as is now in existence. Does any one pretend to believe that this vast mass of gold could be exchanged for the same amount of anything else on the same basis as that of the present? The value of gold would fall as surely as the price of wheat would fall if production was increased tenfold. This is an extravagant supposition, but only extravagant as a matter of degree. The changes due to over-production of gold are slow and insidious, but they are certain.

There is no indication at present that the over-supply of gold will cease in the near future, and, so long as the increase continues, prices of commodities will seek a constantly higher *normal* price.

CHAPTER XIII.

Conclusion.

There is absolutely no hope of success for the speculator who attempts to operate without a good working knowledge of his subject. Any hope of making money by speculative ventures based on tips, inside information, tape reading, chart playing or any of the various methods so frequently employed may as well be set down as an impossible phantom. The man who cannot devote some portion of his time to a study of conditions and the machinery of the market would better let speculation alone entirely. Nor will it be found feasible to merely follow the advice or opinions of some one who makes a study of the subject. Such guidance is valuable provided the recipient understands what is under consideration, what is to be expected marketwise and why such expectations are warranted. A competent adviser may frequently offer suggestions which would have been overlooked, but he should always accompany such advice with the reasons. The adviser may be wrong. No matter how careful he is, every man will fall into error occasionally, and every man who receives advice should examine its merits and foundation before accepting it. I regret to state that a great deal of ignorance is shown by many brokers, letter writers, financial editors and others who pose as advisers. This is in nine cases out of ten due to a lack of study of their subject; an effort to evade hard work and exhaustive examination and supply the omission by alleged inside information or snapshot judgment. They are doing just the thing they should strenuously warn their followers against doing. It is the blind leading the blind. I do not mean to say that financial writers, brokers or editors are ignorant or careless as a class, but there is enough fallacious writing and incompetent opinion from day to day to mislead credulous people and cause considerable loss to those who are not able or willing to judge for themselves the value of the opinions offered. A good many of the newspapers in the smaller cities, and some of them in large cities, make the very serious error of assuming that *anybody* can fill up a financial page, and if the regular editor is absent or incapacitated, his place is frequently filled by a man with no knowledge or special training for his position. The result would be funny, were it not for the damage done to readers who know no more than the writer and who accept the printed pages of a daily paper or market letter at a greater value than they are entitled to. The financial organs are indispensable adjuncts to a comprehensive knowledge of financial affairs and probabilities and we cannot have too many of them or patronize them too liberally, but we should be at all times in a positiou to understand what they are talking about and to reject or disagree with what is unsound in logic or incorrect in statement.

It is not, as many people would have us believe, necessary to devote the entire time to a study of speculation if one is to succeed in such ventures. Thousands of successful merchants, artisans and professional men invest or employ their surplus from time to time in ventures which are either purely speculative or semi-speculative and some of our greatest Wall Street speculators have their fingers on the key-buttons of other enterprises. The idea that a man cannot do more than one thing successfully in this world is a mouldy old maxim which is daily refuted by facts.

The study and research necessary to form correct conclusions as to book values, prospects and the general business outlook is not nearly so staggering or impossible as it might appear at first blush. As has been suggested heretofore, there is frequently a tendency to devote time and study to factors of minor importance which have no power to create or prevent the greater swings of prices. There are so many such factors that an attempt to weigh or study them all results in bewilderment. A great deal of this work is about as valuable as the courses of study in some of our public schools and colleges. Many of these courses of study are about 25 per cent. necessary to an education which will carry an intelligent man or woman creditably through life in any social or business line. The other 75 per cent. is either forgotten or discarded in a few years or is merely embroidery. It is so with the study of finance and probable security movements. A clear understanding of money conditions, crops and our foreign trade, together with a working knowledge of the machinery of the Stock Exchange, constitutes the most important part of such an education. If we start out with these factors as the basis of our curriculum the other necessary branches will be suggested naturally and examination and understanding will follow as a matter of course. Once a clear and comprehensive view of the factors mentioned is obtained the work is reduced to keeping track of progress from day to day or from year to year and supplying oneself continually with the ample and accurate information which James J. Hill says is the first step towards success.

There is another point about this special education which is necessary to successful speculation. Such education broadens the whole scope of knowledge and is valuable in any walk of business life or social intercourse. It is worth having, even if taken up academically and with no intention of ever speculating in securities. For a young man, such a course opens a broader field in any line of business he may undertake. A knowledge of money conditions and the workings of money are necessarry in every line of business and many large concerns gather information as to crop prospects and other important data yearly at considerable expense. Fortunately, the advantages of such knowledge is being more fully recognized by educational institutions, and good periodicals and the sources of information and assistance have been greatly improved and extended in the last few years.

It is astonishing, not to say exasperating, to note the number of people who go about recklessly stating that no amount of study or preparation is useful or necessary in making speculative ventures. They state that the stock market is all a fixed game and that prices do not respond to conditions. Such statements are wholly disproved by precedent. The swings of security prices always have been and always will be based primarily upon fundamentals, and even if misunderstandings, false statements or manipulation should inflate or depress prices noticeably at times, such inflation or depression is always temporary. The people who rashly promulgate the theory of a "fixed-up game," etc., never succeed for any length of time themselves and they do not realize that in following their expressed theory they are eliminating the only possible means of success. But their personal losses are not so much to be deplored as the evil effects of their fulminations in influencing other people to abjure proper investigation and study, and go blindly to loss and possible ruin by the fatal roads of ignorance and prejudice. Any retailer or publisher of financial works will confirm the statement that the greatest percentage of his books go to well-to-do and successful men or to young men with a promising future, and the tendency to read and study such works is growing so rapidly that we may hope in time to see the old idea dispelled that, of all the forms of speculation, that in securities is the only one universally stigmatized as gambling. The only reason for this special characterization is that for years people have gambled in securities and called their *gambling* speculation. The term is abused by reversing this process and calling *speculation* gambling.

A large number of people constantly "take flyers" in securities on some word of advice or whispered tip. Sometimes they make money on such a venture, which is unfortunate, as it leads to further transactions and final loss. It is all right to take advice—all you can get of it—but get the reasons and be sure they are logical and based on correct statements. No man on earth can build up a fortune for you in speculation if you do not know what you are about. Even if the advice offered is sincere and correct, if its recipient is ignorant of the possibilities and vagaries of the market, he will secretly over-extend himself, or be frightened from his position by events, the importance of which he cannot judge, or will become confused by the conflicting advice he is sure to receive from other sources at times. He cannot be free from such dangers except through a personal understanding of the subject. A man who cannot read the salient points of a railroad report, or who has no clear conception of the forces which make and break security prices, has no business in the stock market. If he makes a profit at first he will keep on speculating in an attempt to get rich and if he loses he will keep on speculating in an attempt to get even. The outcome will be the same in every case.

Speculation is a business, with certain rules and laws, and it is necessary to understand the business if we are to succeed at it. It is not a get-rich-quick business. The rewards are sometimes very large, but no larger than in other lines of business. The losses are greater and more numerous than in other lines simply because it is the only business on earth an intelligent man would ever consider entering with no knowledge, special equipment or natural ability in that direction. No truer statement was ever made than that many a man has come to Wall Street to get rich and has been ruined, while on the other hand many a man has come to Wall Street to make a fair return on capital and become rich.

Nothing will more greatly and pleasantly surprise the man who studies speculation correctly than the accuracy and facility with which he will find himself arriving at correct conclusions and profitable results. Nothing will more surprise the man who does not approach the business properly than the rapidity with which he will lose his money. Yet in either case the outcome is quite according to natural laws and would be really surprising if it turned out otherwise. The speculator should keep in mind and rigidly adhere to the following speculative don'ts.

Don't speculate on tips or alleged inside information. Tips are too frequently guesswork and when "information" is distributed to people gratuitously it has either ceased to be "inside information," in which case the market effects have been discounted, or the news is distributed for an ulterior purpose.

Don't speculate on advice unless it is accompanied by the reasons on which the advice is based, and then only if you are capable of weighing such reasons competently.

Don't be either credulous or prejudiced. One is about as bad as the other.

Don't over-speculate. This is the biggest don't of all. Take what you can safely carry through a decline occasioned by accident or manipulation; or better still, be prepared to take advantage of such a decline by increasing holdings.

Don't expect to get rich quick. You will be disappointed. Accept returns when it appears best to sell, whether they are large or small.

Don't sell merely because you have a profit. Conditions may be such that further profits are more certain than at the time of the initial commitment.

Don't hang on to a losing proposition in the hope that something will occur to pull you out. If you find your original reasons for buying to have been erroneous or if conditions change and upset the original calculation, take your loss at once and await another oppportunity.

Don't take a loss simply because the market does not at once favor you or because of a decline which occurs without any change in prospects or conditions. If your original deductions are correct the market will come back to you in time.

Don't sell as soon as you "get even," after a long period of reversal and waiting. That may be just the time to hold on. Be governed by present conditions and prospects, not by the intangible and unimportant fact that you are "even."

Don't gamble on stop loss orders, chart systems or tape appearances. Don't gamble at all —speculate.

Don't hang over a ticker or spend your time watching the blackboard. It does no good at all and frequently results in confusion and apprehension by magnifying the importance of the inevitable and insignificant fluctuations which are a daily component of every market.

Don't speculate at all unless you are willing to devote a reasonable amount of time to the study of prospects and conditions. Nothing else will do.

The Pitfalls of Speculation

BY THOMAS GIBSON

In this volume the author has endeavored to discuss as simply as is possible, the salient factors of speculation and investment. The Table of Contents, following the introduction, treats of:

Ignorance.
Over-Speculation, etc.
Manipulation.
Accidents.
Business Methods in Speculation.
Market Technicalities.
Tips.
Mechanical Speculation.
Short Selling.
What 500 Speculative Accounts Showed.
Grain Speculation.
Suggestions as to Intelligent Methods.
Conclusion.

BOUND IN CLOTH, 146 PAGES. PRICE, $1.

THE GIBSON PUBLISHING CO.
29 Broadway, New York

The Cycles of Speculation

BY THOMAS GIBSON

This book enters a little further into the influences bearing on price changes, than does the "Pitfalls of Speculation," described on the preceding page.

The Table of Contents introduces as bearing upon the subject:

Bound in cloth, 183 pages; uniform size and binding with "Pitfalls of Speculation." Price, $1.50.

THE GIBSON PUBLISHING CO.

29 Broadway,   New York

SD - #0072 - 110825 - C0 - 229/152/9 - PB - 9781330807682 - Gloss Lamination